CLASSIC
POLYHEDRA
ORIGAMI

CLASSIC
POLYHEDRA
ORIGAMI

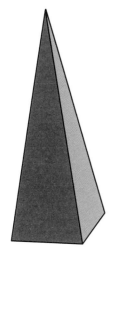

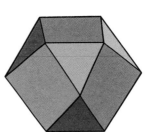
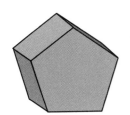
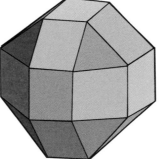

JOHN MONTROLL

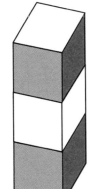

Dover Publications, Inc.
New York

To John, Jean, Lizzy, and Michelle

Introduction

 olyhedra are some of the most beautiful geometric shapes imaginable. The ancient Greeks and other cultures believed polyhedra had mystical powers. Each shape seems to radiate a different feeling. In this collection you will make many discoveries as you uncover the secrets of folding polyhedra. It is very satisfying to fold your own, each from a single square sheet of paper.

There are 33 polyhedra in this collection. You will learn to fold the five Platonic solids—the tetrahedron, cube, octahedron, icosahedron, and dodecahedron. Also included are several pyramids, prisms, antiprisms, Archimedean Solids, and Catalan Solids. The models have been organized in groups of related polyhedra. Each group is ordered by level of difficulty, and each group itself becomes progressively more difficult. I strive to find the most efficient designs with respect to ease in folding, good use of the paper, and good locks. Please check online for more of my titles on this subject.

The diagrams conform to the internationally approved Randlett-Yoshizawa style. Although any square paper can be used for the projects in this book, the best material is origami paper. The colored side of origami paper is represented by the shadings in the diagrams. Origami supplies can be found in arts and craft shops, or visit Dover Publications online at www.doverpublications.com, or OrigamiUSA at www.origami-usa.org. Large sheets are easier to use than small ones.

Many people helped make this origami polyhedra symphony possible. I thank Robert Lang for his efficeint folding sequences. Thanks to my editors, Jan Polish and Charley Montroll. Of course, I also thank the many folders who proof read the diagrams.

John Montroll

www.johnmontroll.com

Contents

★ Simple
★★ Intermediate
★★★ Complex
★★★★ Very Complex

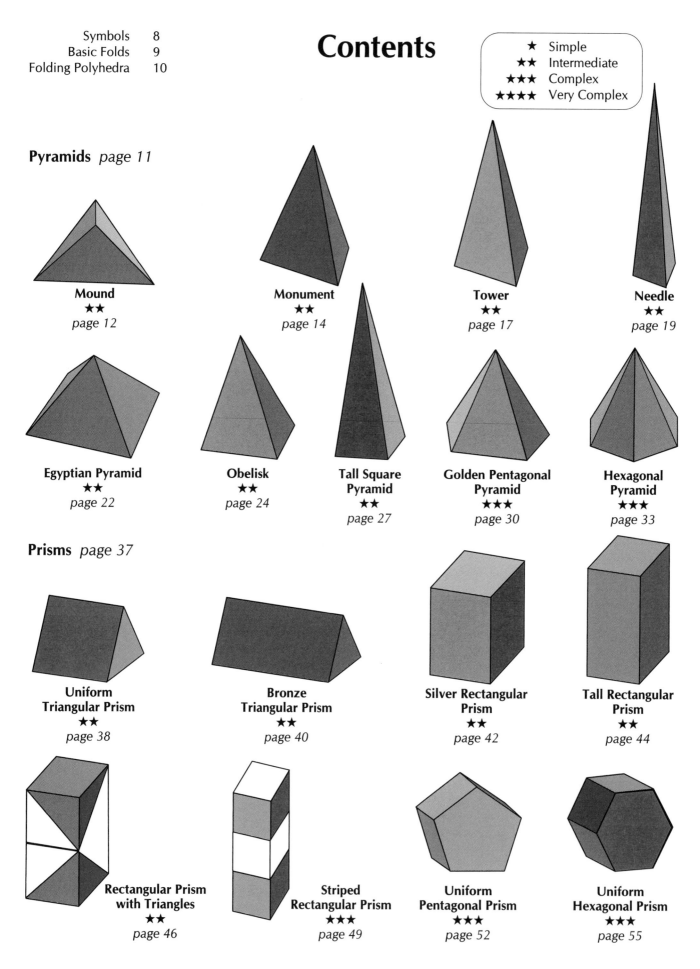

Pyramids *page 11*

Mound
★★
page 12

Monument
★★
page 14

Tower
★★
page 17

Needle
★★
page 19

Egyptian Pyramid
★★
page 22

Obelisk
★★
page 24

Tall Square Pyramid
★★
page 27

Golden Pentagonal Pyramid
★★★
page 30

Hexagonal Pyramid
★★★
page 33

Prisms *page 37*

Uniform Triangular Prism
★★
page 38

Bronze Triangular Prism
★★
page 40

Silver Rectangular Prism
★★
page 42

Tall Rectangular Prism
★★
page 44

Rectangular Prism with Triangles
★★
page 46

Striped Rectangular Prism
★★★
page 49

Uniform Pentagonal Prism
★★★
page 52

Uniform Hexagonal Prism
★★★
page 55

Antiprisms *page 58*

  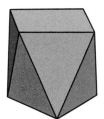  

Tall Triangular Antiprism
★★★
page 59

Uniform Square Antiprism
★★★
page 62

Tall Square Antiprism
★★★
page 66

Golden Pentagonal Antiprism
★★★
page 70

Uniform Hexagonal Antiprism
★★★
page 74

The Platonic Solids *page 78*

Tetrahedron
★
page 79

Cube
★★
page 81

Octahedron
★★
page 83

Icosahedron
★★★
page 86

Dodecahedron
★★★★
page 90

Archimedean and Catalan Solids *page 96*

  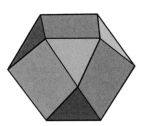

Truncated Tetrahedron
★★★
page 97

Triakis Tetrahedron
★★★
page 100

Cuboctahedron
★★★
page 104

 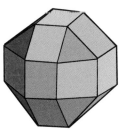 

Dimpled Rhombic Dodecahedron
★★★
page 108

Rhombicuboctahedron
★★★
page 112

Triakis Cube
★★★★
page 116

Symbols

Lines

— — — — — — — — — Valley fold, fold in front.

— · · — · · — · · — · · — Mountain fold, fold behind.

———————————— Crease line.

·· X-ray or guide line.

Arrows

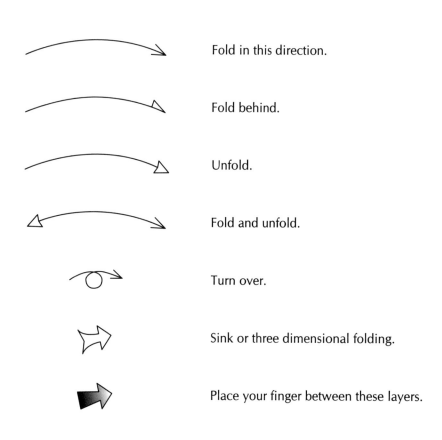

Fold in this direction.

Fold behind.

Unfold.

Fold and unfold.

Turn over.

Sink or three dimensional folding.

Place your finger between these layers.

Basic Folds

Squash Fold.

In a squash fold, some paper is opened and then made flat. The shaded arrow shows where to place your finger.

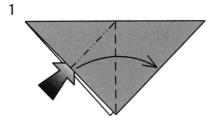

Squash-fold.

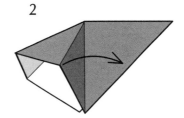

A 3D intermediate step.

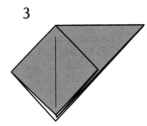

Inside Reverse Fold.

In an inside reverse fold, some paper is folded between layers. Here are two examples.

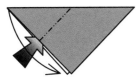

Reverse-fold.

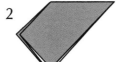

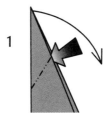

Reverse-fold.

Sink Fold.

In a sink fold, some of the paper without edges is folded inside. To do this fold, much of the model must be unfolded.

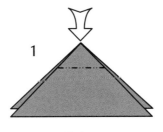

Sink.

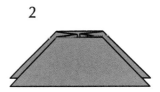

Folding Polyhedra

Folding polyhedra from a single square sheet of paper so that they hold together requires different and new ways of folding. Because of this new adventure, I recommend you start with the simple or intermediate models shown below.

Polyhedra require extensive use of three-dimensional folding. During that stage, be careful to understand how to interpret the valley and mountain fold lines. Where a mountain fold line typically means to fold behind, it could now refer to folding slightly behind. Another challenge during the three-dimensional folding is that the model might want to come apart and you wish for several extra hands.

Symmetry plays an important part in the folding procedure. Most of the models is this collection have even, odd, even/odd, or square symmetry. For even symmetry, the crease pattern shows a mirror image around a center line. Several pyramids have even symmetry. For odd symmetry, the crease pattern is the same when rotated 180°. The icosahedron, dodecahedron, and several antiprisms use odd symmetry. Even/odd is for the models with both forms, found in some of the prisms. For square symmetry, the crease pattern is the same when rotated 90°, as in the octahedron and triakis cube. Knowing symmetry simplifies the folding.

Here are the typical stages in folding my polyhedra:

1. Stage 1 is finding the location of a landmark that is the key to folding the rest of the model. In some models this is found immediately and easily, while in others it could take over a page.

2. Stage 2 is in making all the initial creases. Often only small segments of a fold are creased. This is typically a couple of pages of simply folding and unfolding—the calm before the storm.

3. Then comes stage 3 where the main folding begins. The model becomes three-dimensional and the shape is realized.

4. Finally, stage 4 is the locking, tucking, or whatever it takes to close or finish the polyhedra. In some it is an easy tuck, but in others it takes some juggling to get all the loose ends to cooperate.

Some simple and intermediate models:

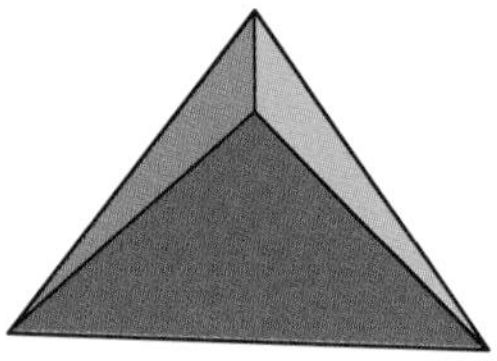

Mound
page 12

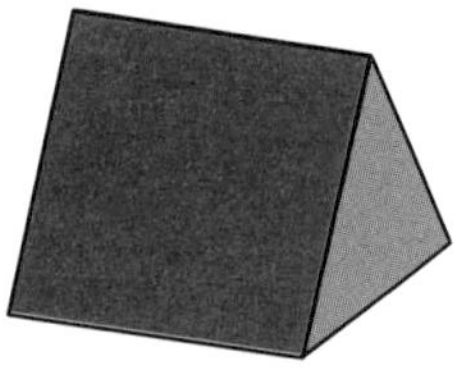

**Uniform
Triangular Prism**
page 38

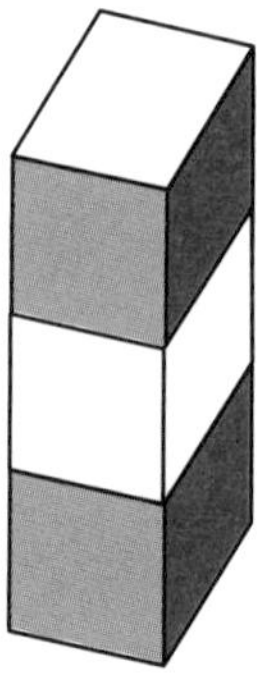

**Striped
Rectangular Prism**
page 49

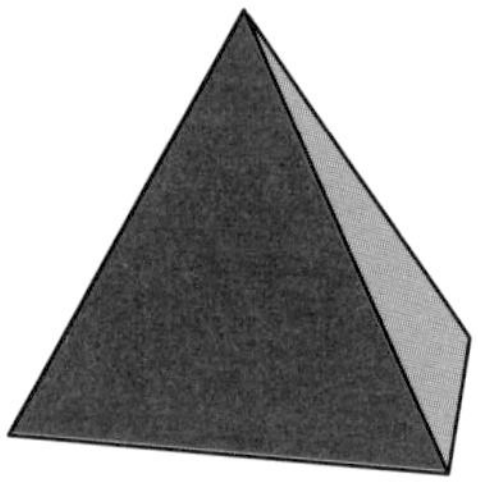

Tetrahedron
page 79

Cube
page 81

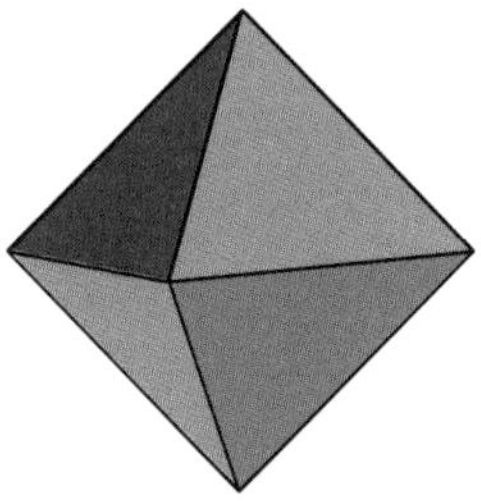

Octahedron
page 83

Pyramids

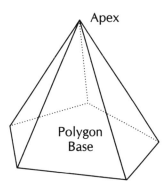

Apex

Polygon
Base

A pyramid is a polyhedron formed by connecting a polygon
base at the bottom to a point at the top, the apex. Triangles
are formed from the edge of the base and the apex.

Here is a collection of pyramids including the tetrahedron
from the Platonic Solids section. These range from triangular
to hexagonal bases and from low to high.

Triangular Pyramids.

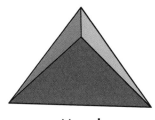    

Mound   **Tetrahedron**   **Monument**   **Tower**   **Needle**

More Pyramids.

Egyptian Pyramid   **Obelisk**   **Tall Square
Pyramid**   **Golden Pentagonal
Pyramid**   **Hexagonal
Pyramid**

Mound

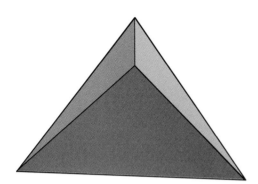 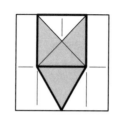 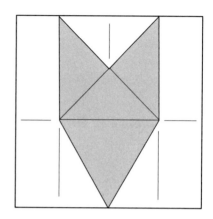

This stout pyramid is formed from a triangular base and three isosceles right triangles. The crease pattern shows that even symmetry is used since the left and right sides are mirror images. The small drawing shows that the crease pattern includes a square above an equilateral triangle, spanning the length of the square paper.

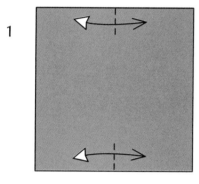

1 Fold and unfold at the top and bottom.

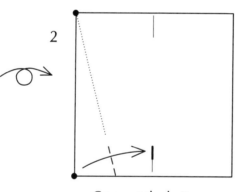

2 Crease at the bottom.

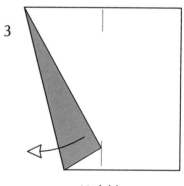

3 Unfold.

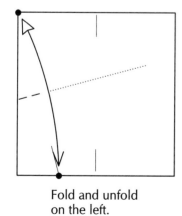

4 Fold and unfold on the left.

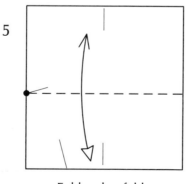

5 Fold and unfold.

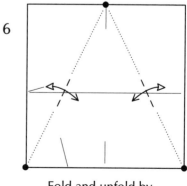

6 Fold and unfold by the horizontal crease.

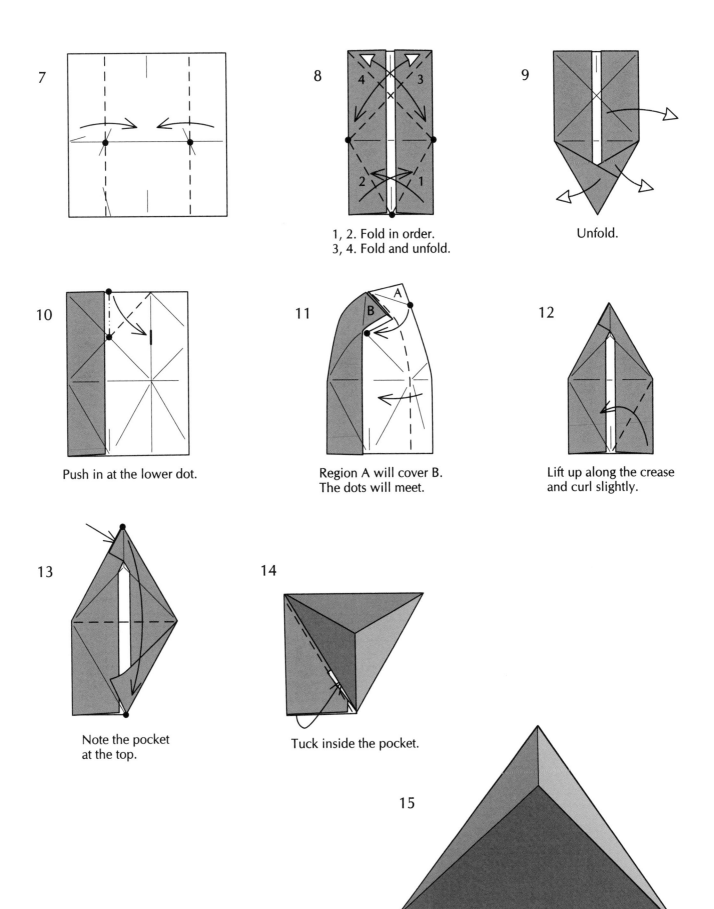

7

8

1, 2. Fold in order.
3, 4. Fold and unfold.

9

Unfold.

10

Push in at the lower dot.

11

Region A will cover B.
The dots will meet.

12

Lift up along the crease
and curl slightly.

13

Note the pocket
at the top.

14

Tuck inside the pocket.

15

Mound

Monument

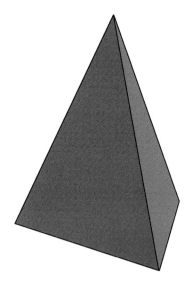

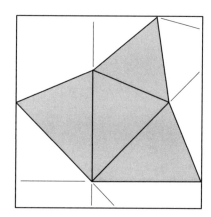

This pyramid is formed from a triangular base and three isosceles triangles, with an apex angle of 45°. This is one of the few models where the crease pattern is not symmetric.

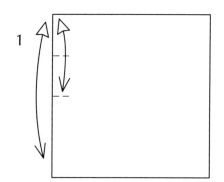

1 Fold and unfold on the left to find the quarter mark.

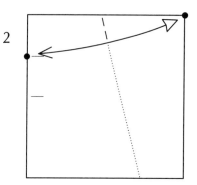

2 Fold and unfold at the top.

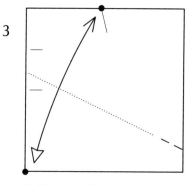

3 Fold and unfold on the right.

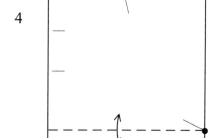

4 Fold and unfold.

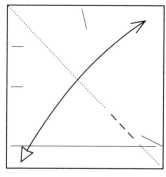

5 Fold and unfold.

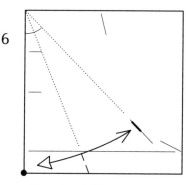

6 Fold and unfold at the bottom.

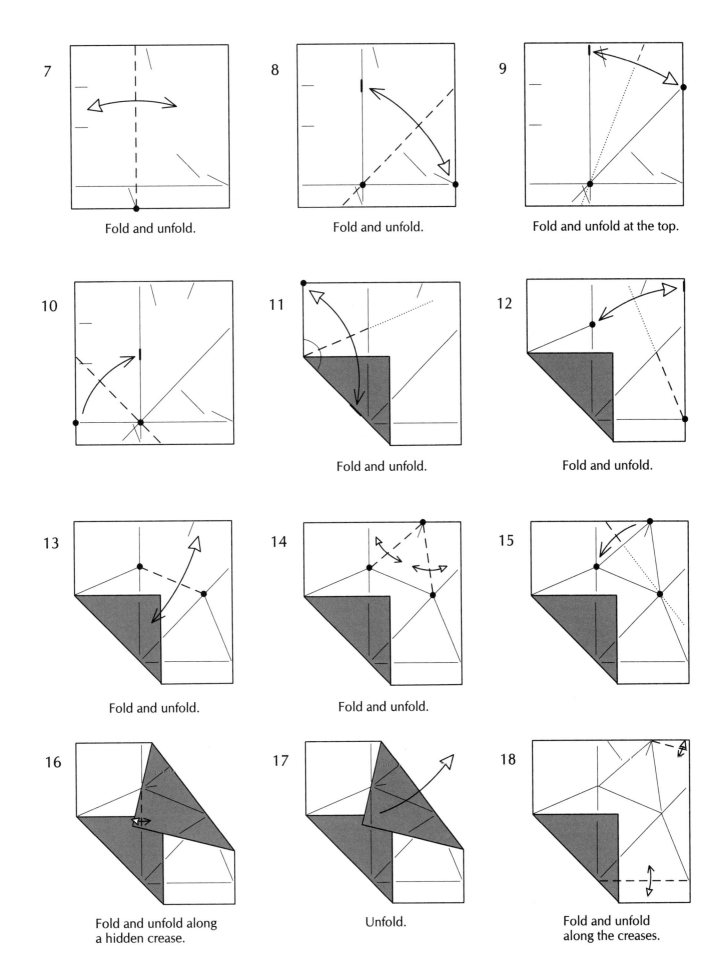

7 Fold and unfold.

8 Fold and unfold.

9 Fold and unfold at the top.

10

11 Fold and unfold.

12 Fold and unfold.

13 Fold and unfold.

14 Fold and unfold.

15

16 Fold and unfold along a hidden crease.

17 Unfold.

18 Fold and unfold along the creases.

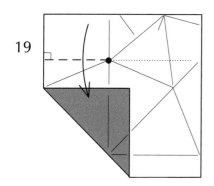

19

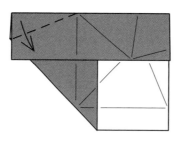

20

Fold along a hidden crease.

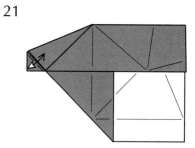

21

Fold and unfold.

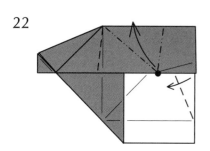

22

Lift up at the dot.

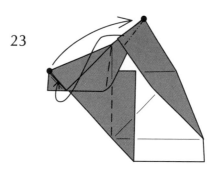

23

The dots will meet. Tuck
the tab under some layers.

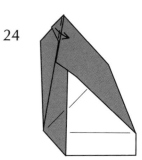

24

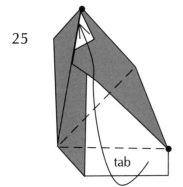

25

Tuck the tab inside. The tab curls
by the dots. Rotate the equilateral
triangle to the bottom.

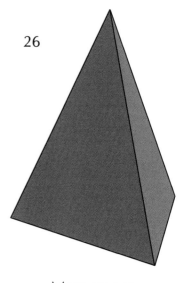

26

Monument

Tower

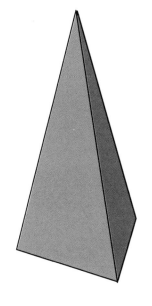

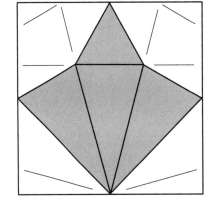

This tall pyramid is formed from a triangular base and three isosceles triangles, with an apex angle of 30°. This model uses even symmetry.

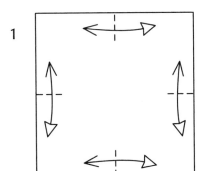

1

Fold and unfold to find the centers on each side.

2

3

Fold the left edge to the dot.

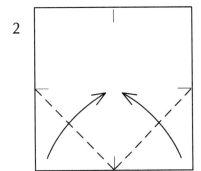

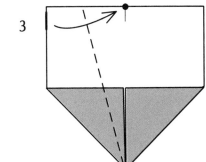

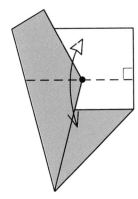

4

Fold and unfold.

5

Fold and unfold.

6

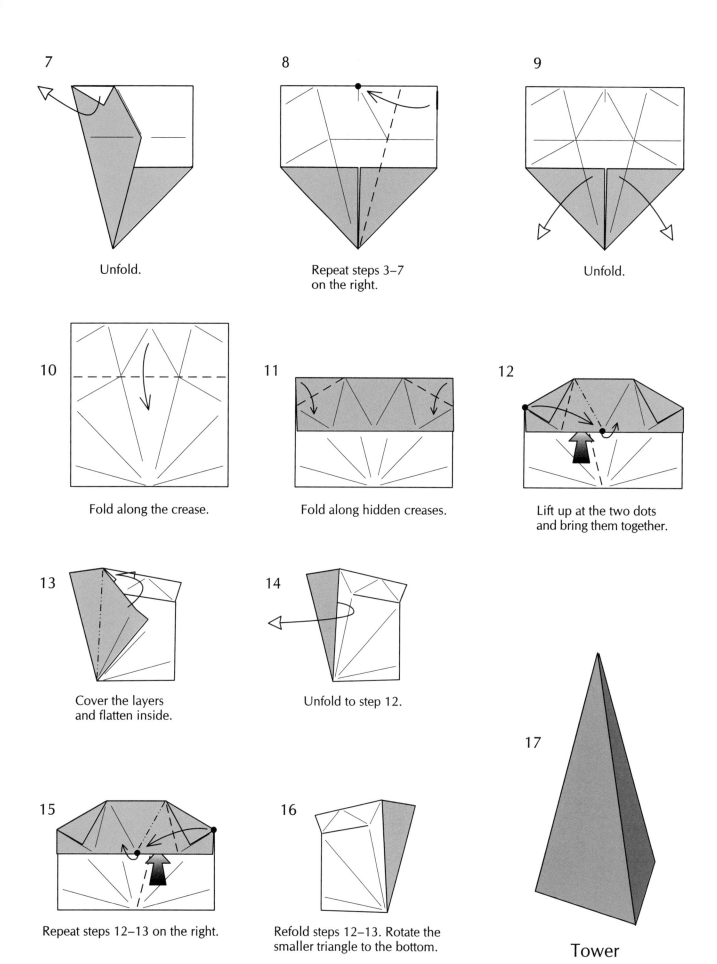

7

Unfold.

8

Repeat steps 3–7
on the right.

9

Unfold.

10

Fold along the crease.

11

Fold along hidden creases.

12

Lift up at the two dots
and bring them together.

13

Cover the layers
and flatten inside.

14

Unfold to step 12.

15

Repeat steps 12–13 on the right.

16

Refold steps 12–13. Rotate the
smaller triangle to the bottom.

17

Tower

Needle

This extremely pointy pyramid is formed from a triangular base and three isosceles triangles, with an apex angle of 15°. Even symmetry is used.

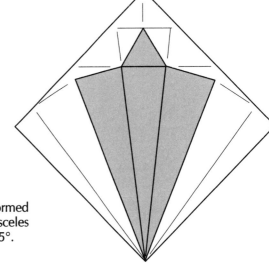

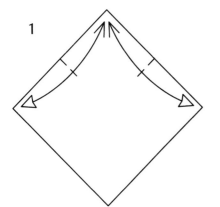

1

Fold and unfold in half on the edges.

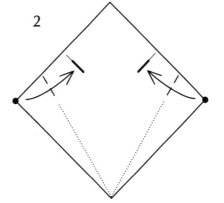

2

Bring the corners to the creases, folding near the top.

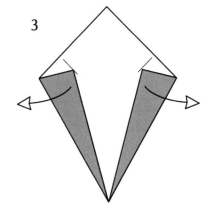

3

Unfold.

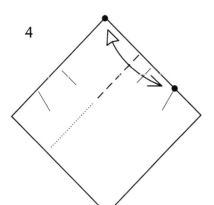

4

Fold and unfold.

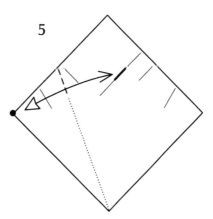

5

Fold and unfold the corner to the crease. Crease near the top.

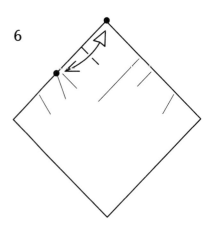

6

Fold and unfold.

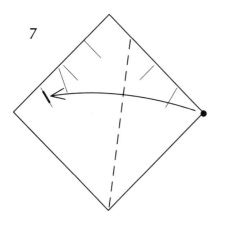
7

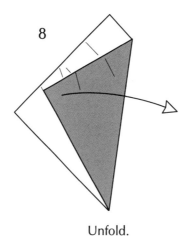
8

Unfold.

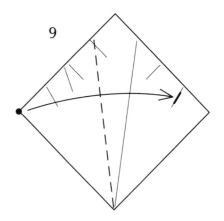
9

Repeat steps 7–8 in
the opposite direction.

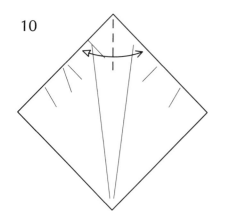
10

Fold and unfold at the top.

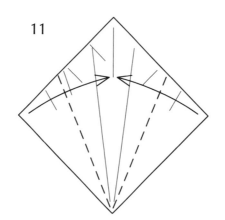
11

Kite-fold.

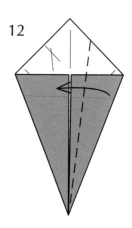
12

Fold along a partially
hidden crease.

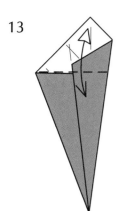
13

Fold and unfold.

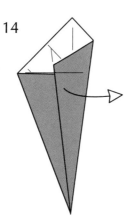
14

Unfold.

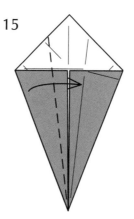
15

Repeat steps
12–14 on the left.

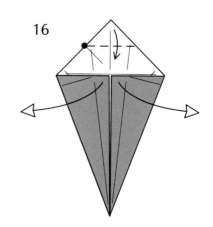
16

Unfold at the sides.

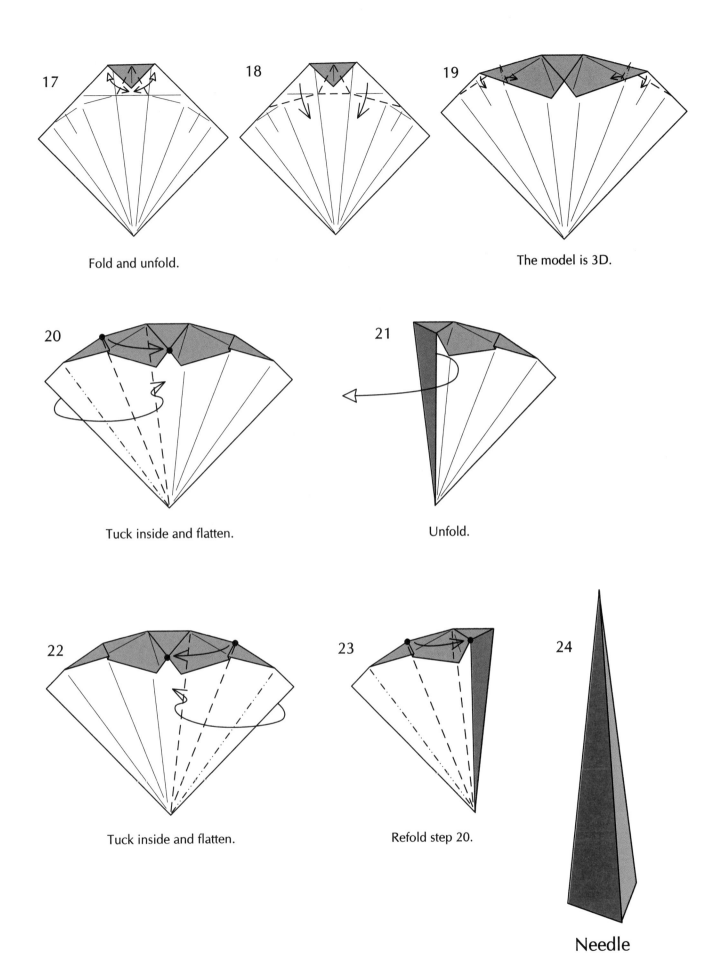

17

Fold and unfold.

18

19

The model is 3D.

20

Tuck inside and flatten.

21

Unfold.

22

Tuck inside and flatten.

23

Refold step 20.

24

Needle

Egyptian Pyramid

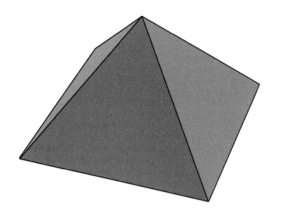

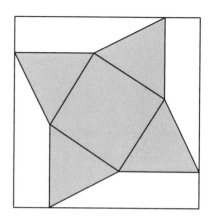

This model is proportional to some of the Egyptian pyramids. The four isosceles triangles have a base of 2 units and height of phi units. Phi, φ, is the golden mean, $(\sqrt{5} + 1)/2 = 1.618034$.

The golden mean, φ, occurs in nature and is associated with beauty.

The crease pattern shows that this design has square symmetry, that is, when the crease pattern is rotated 90°, it remains the same. This simplifies the folding and also leads to the twist lock, the last step of the model. When designing polyhedra, square symmetry is the best choice when possible.

1

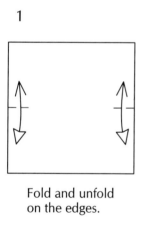

Fold and unfold
on the edges.

2

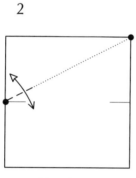

Fold and unfold
on the left.

3

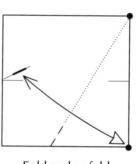

Fold and unfold
on the bottom.

4

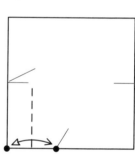

Fold and unfold.
Rotate 180°.

5

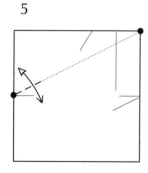

Repeat steps 2–4.

6

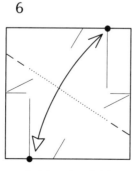

Fold and unfold
on the edges.

7

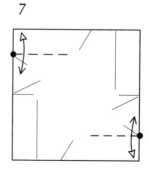

Fold and unfold.

8

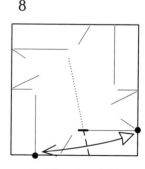

Fold and unfold
by the bottom.

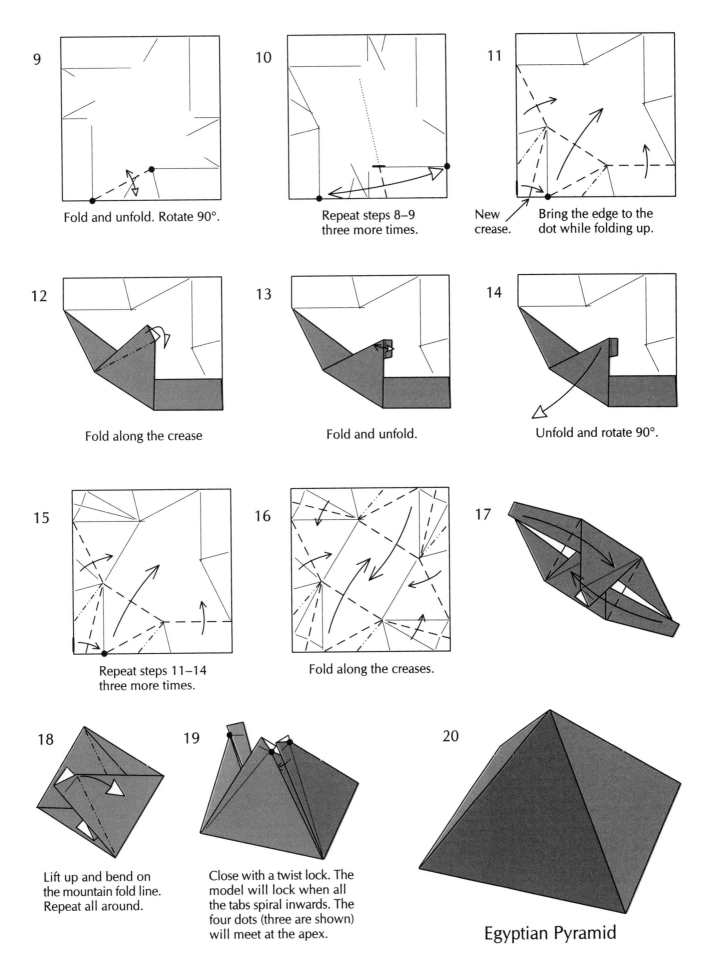

9 Fold and unfold. Rotate 90°.

10 Repeat steps 8–9 three more times.

11 New crease. Bring the edge to the dot while folding up.

12 Fold along the crease

13 Fold and unfold.

14 Unfold and rotate 90°.

15 Repeat steps 11–14 three more times.

16 Fold along the creases.

17

18 Lift up and bend on the mountain fold line. Repeat all around.

19 Close with a twist lock. The model will lock when all the tabs spiral inwards. The four dots (three are shown) will meet at the apex.

20 Egyptian Pyramid

Obelisk

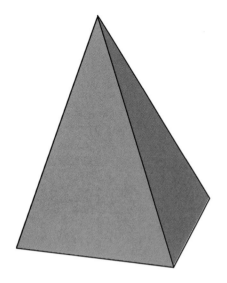

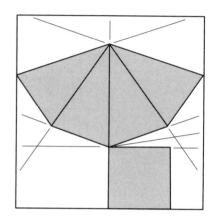

This pyramid is formed from a square base and four isosceles triangles, with an apex angle of 36°. The crease pattern is close to even symmetry.

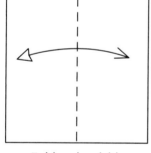

1

Fold and unfold.

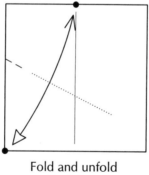

2

Fold and unfold on the left.

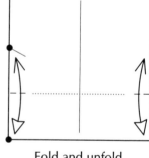

3

Fold and unfold on the edges.

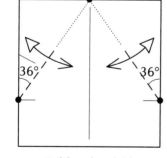

4

Fold and unfold in the middle.

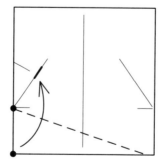

5

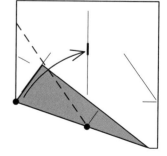

6

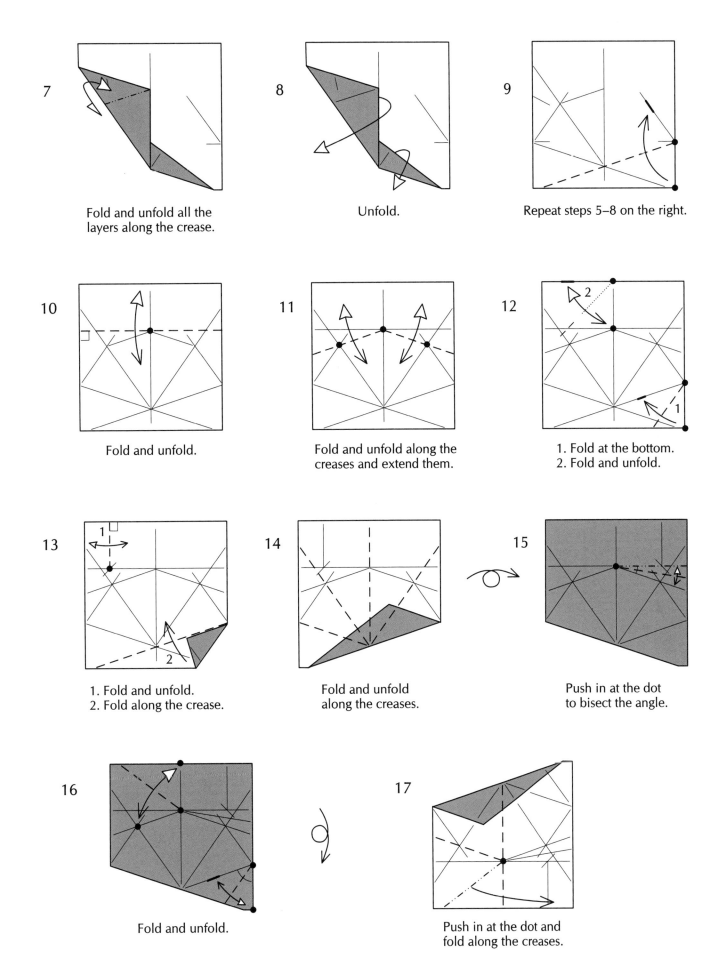

7 Fold and unfold all the layers along the crease.

8 Unfold.

9 Repeat steps 5–8 on the right.

10 Fold and unfold.

11 Fold and unfold along the creases and extend them.

12
1. Fold at the bottom.
2. Fold and unfold.

13
1. Fold and unfold.
2. Fold along the crease.

14 Fold and unfold along the creases.

15 Push in at the dot to bisect the angle.

16 Fold and unfold.

17 Push in at the dot and fold along the creases.

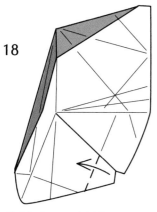

18

Fold along a hidden crease.

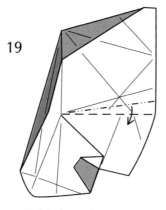

19

Fold along the creases.

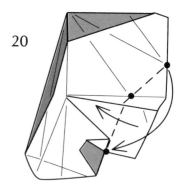

20

Push in at the center dot. The other dots will meet.

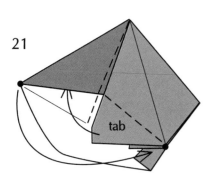

21

Tuck the tab inside.

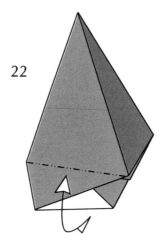

22

Fold and unfold.

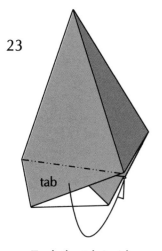

23

Tuck the tab inside.

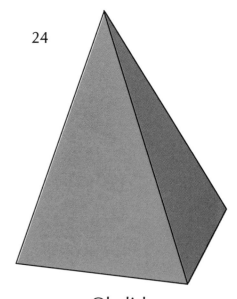

24

Obelisk

Tall Square Pyramid

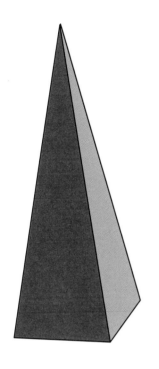

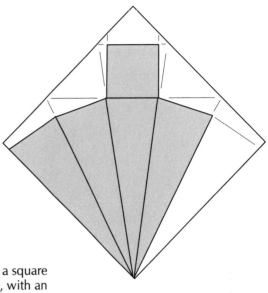

This tall pyramid is formed from a square base and four isosceles triangles, with an apex angle of 18°. The crease pattern shows mainly even symmetry.

1

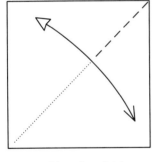

Fold and unfold by the top.

2

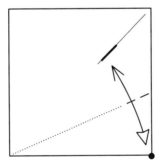

Fold and unfold on the right.

3

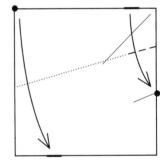

Bring the top edge to the right dot and the top left corner to the bottom edge. Crease on the right.

4

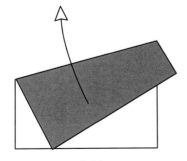

Unfold.

5

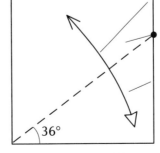

36°

Fold and unfold.

6

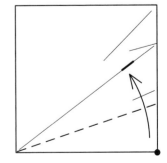

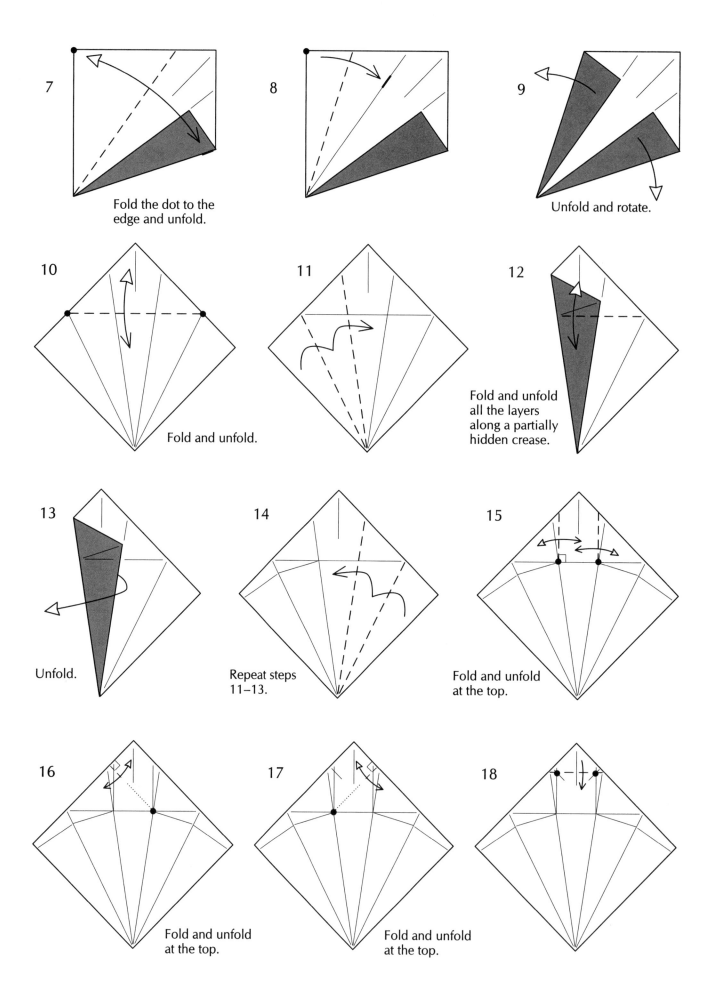

7 Fold the dot to the edge and unfold.

8

9 Unfold and rotate.

10 Fold and unfold.

11

12 Fold and unfold all the layers along a partially hidden crease.

13 Unfold.

14 Repeat steps 11–13.

15 Fold and unfold at the top.

16 Fold and unfold at the top.

17 Fold and unfold at the top.

18

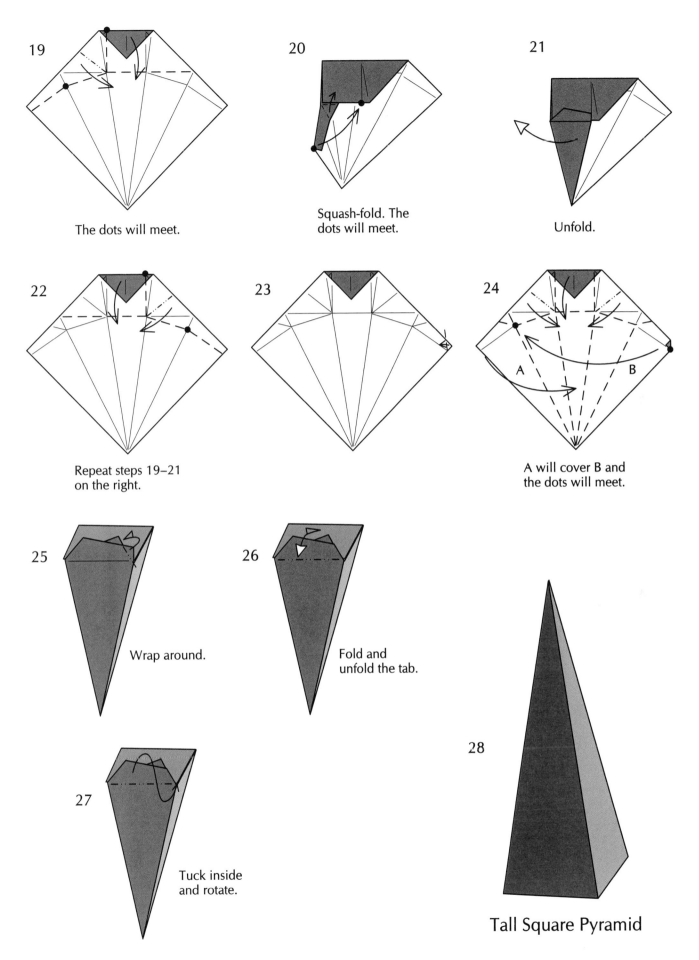

19

The dots will meet.

20

Squash-fold. The
dots will meet.

21

Unfold.

22

Repeat steps 19–21
on the right.

23

24

A will cover B and
the dots will meet.

25

Wrap around.

26

Fold and
unfold the tab.

27

Tuck inside
and rotate.

28

Tall Square Pyramid

Golden Pentagonal Pyramid

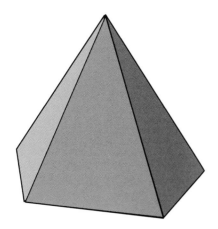

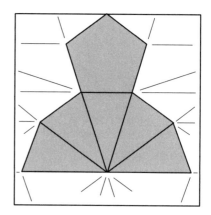

This pyramid is formed from a pentagonal base and five isosceles triangles, with an apex angle of 36°. The crease pattern shows even symmetry.

1

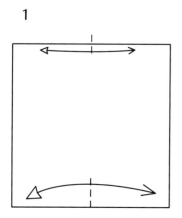

Fold and unfold. Make a small crease at the top and a slightly larger one at the bottom.

2

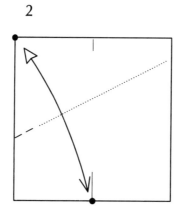

Fold and unfold on the left.

3

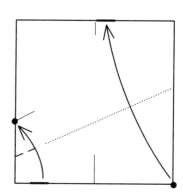

Bring the lower dot to the top edge and the bottom edge to the dot on the left. Crease on the left.

4

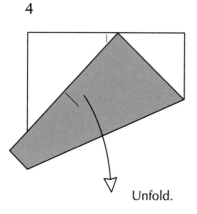

Unfold.

5

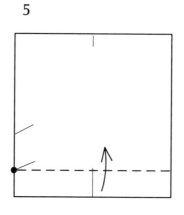

6

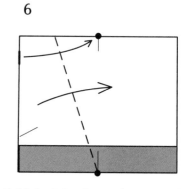

Fold the left edge to the upper dot.

7

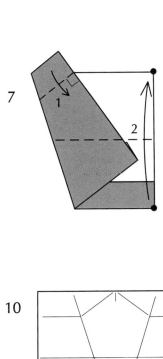

8

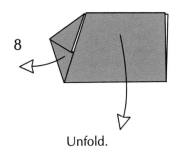

Unfold.

9

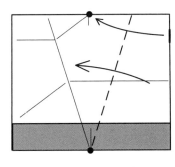

Repeat steps 6–8
on the right.

10

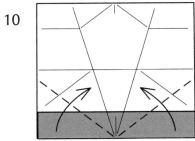

11

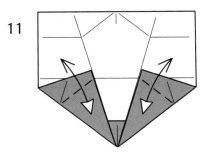

Fold and unfold all the layers
along hidden creases.

12

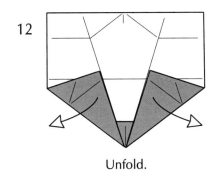

Unfold.

13

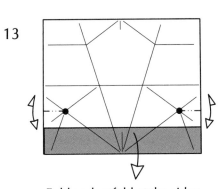

Fold and unfold at the sides
and unfold at the bottom.

14

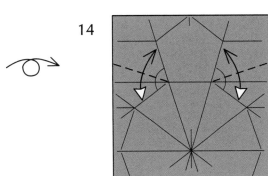

Fold and unfold to bisect the
angles. Turn over and rotate 180°.

15

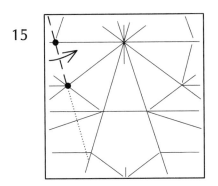

Fold along the crease between the dots.

16

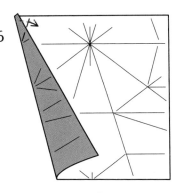

Fold along the crease.

17

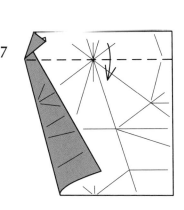

Golden Pentagonal Pyramid 31

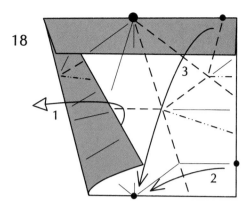

18

The model will become 3D. Unfold on the lower left. Bring the dots on the right to the lower dot. The large dot will be at the top of the pyramid.

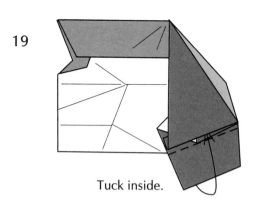

19

Tuck inside.

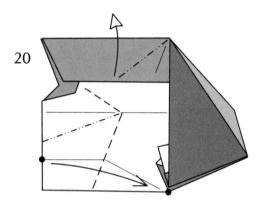

20

Fold at the bottom and unfold at the top.

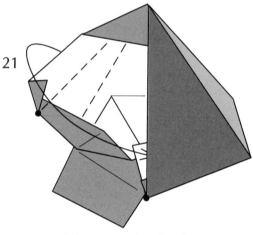

21

Wrap around and tuck inside. The dots will meet.

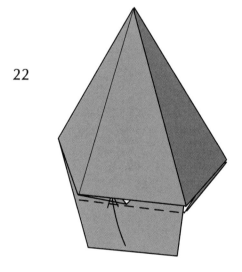

22

Tuck inside.

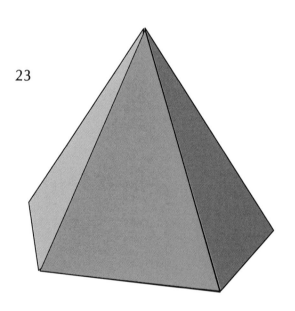

23

Golden Pentagonal Pyramid

Hexagonal Pyramid

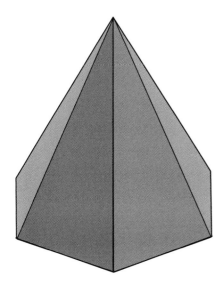

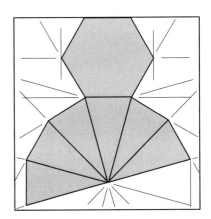

This pyramid is formed from a hexagonal base and six isosceles triangles, with an apex angle of 30°. The crease pattern shows mainly even symmetry.

1

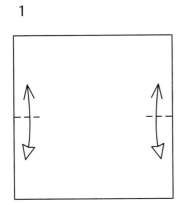

Fold and unfold
on the edges.

2

Crease at the top.

3

Unfold.

4

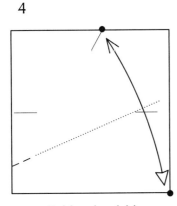

Fold and unfold
on the left.

5

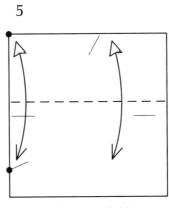

Fold and unfold.

6

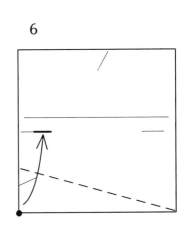

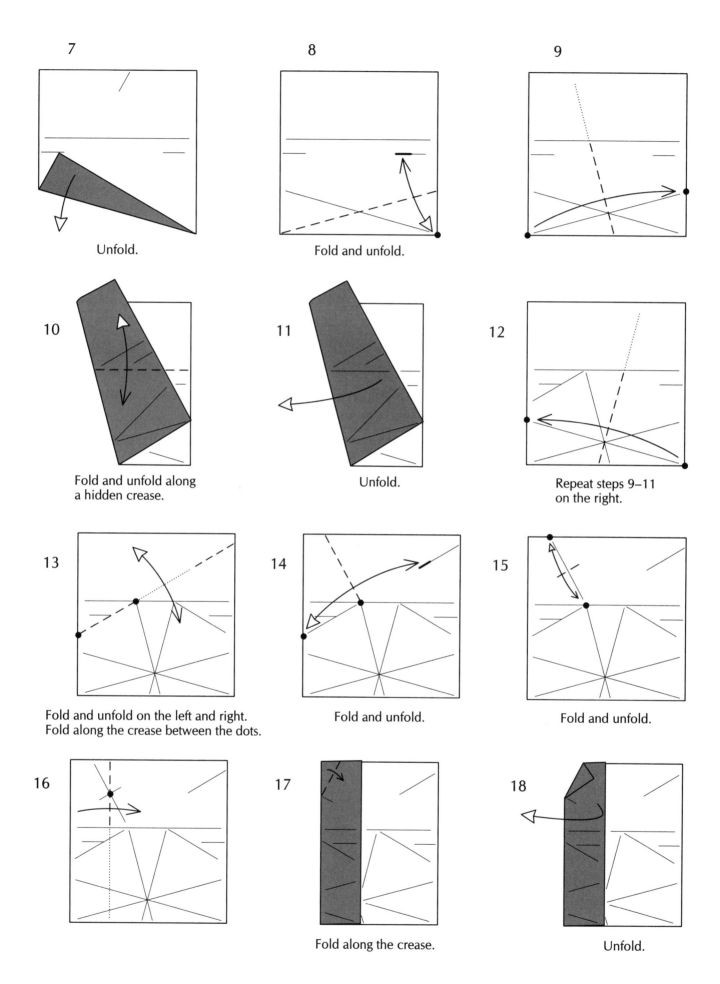

7

Unfold.

8

Fold and unfold.

9

10

Fold and unfold along
a hidden crease.

11

Unfold.

12

Repeat steps 9–11
on the right.

13

Fold and unfold on the left and right.
Fold along the crease between the dots.

14

Fold and unfold.

15

Fold and unfold.

16

17

Fold along the crease.

18

Unfold.

19

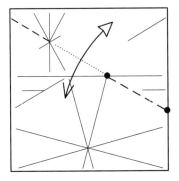

Repeat steps 13–18
on the right.

20

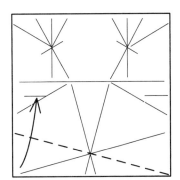

21

22

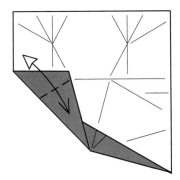

Fold and unfold along
a hidden crease.

23

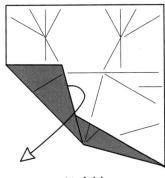

Unfold.

24

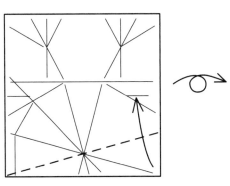

Repeat steps 20–23
on the right.

25

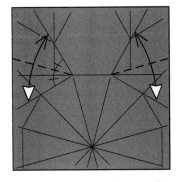

Fold and unfold to bisect the
angles. Turn over and rotate 180°.

26

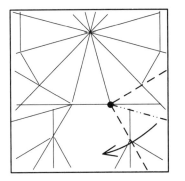

Push in at the dot.

27

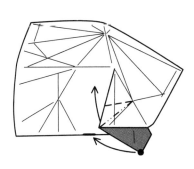

28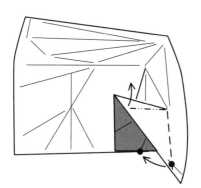

29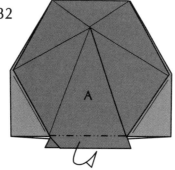

Repeat steps 26–28
on the left.

30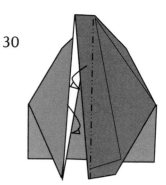

31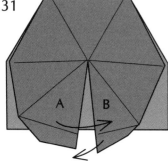

Region A will cover region B.

32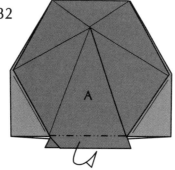

Tuck inside.

33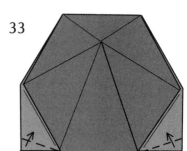

Fold at roughly one-third
of the angle.

34

Tuck inside.

35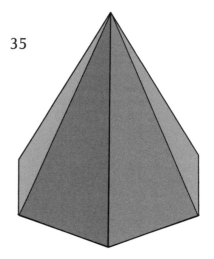

Hexagonal Pyramid

Prisms

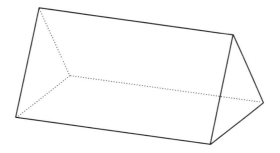

A prism is a polyhedron where two congruent polygons are connected by parallelograms. A uniform prism is composed of two congruent polygons connected by squares.

Here is a collection of prisms, including the cube from the Platonic Solids section. There are also some color pattern rectangular prisms.

Uniform Prisms.

**Uniform
Triangular Prism**

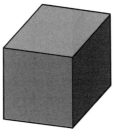

Cube

**Uniform
Pentagonal Prism**

**Uniform
Hexagonal Prism**

More Prisms.

**Bronze
Triangular Prism**

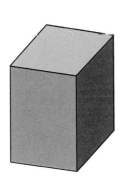

**Silver Rectangular
Prism**

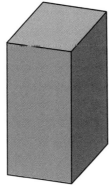

**Tall Rectangular
Prism**

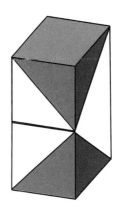

**Rectangular Prism
with Triangles**

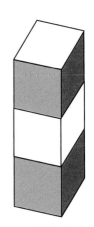

**Striped
Rectangular Prism**

Uniform Triangular Prism

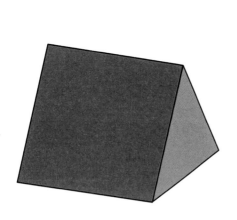

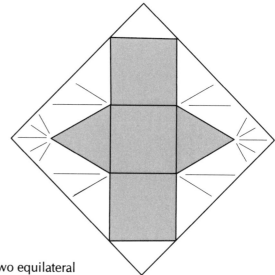

This triangular prism is composed of two equilateral triangles and three squares. All the prisms in the collection use even symmetry. This one is even/odd. It is even since the left and right sides are mirror images, but also odd because the pattern is the same when rotated 180°.

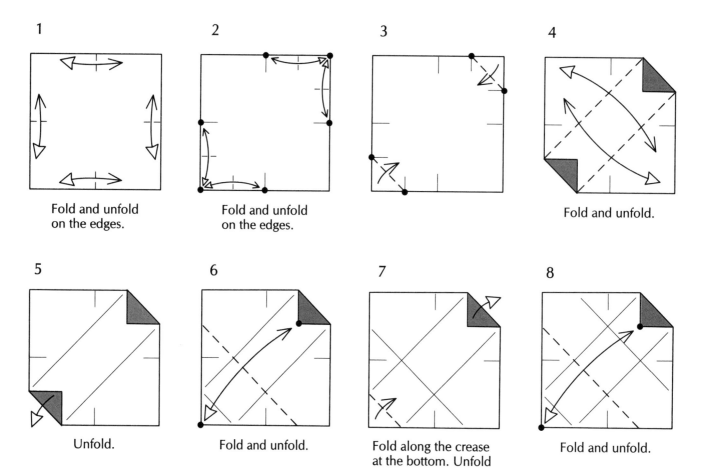

1

Fold and unfold
on the edges.

2

Fold and unfold
on the edges.

3

4

Fold and unfold.

5

Unfold.

6

Fold and unfold.

7

Fold along the crease
at the bottom. Unfold
at the top. Rotate 180°.

8

Fold and unfold.

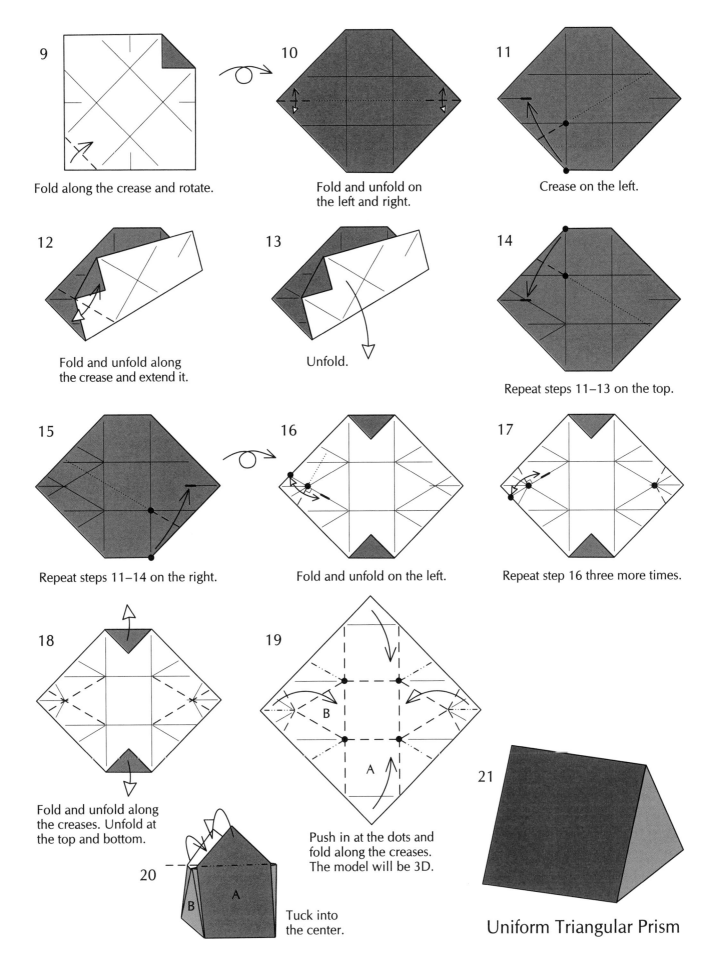

9 Fold along the crease and rotate.

10 Fold and unfold on the left and right.

11 Crease on the left.

12 Fold and unfold along the crease and extend it.

13 Unfold.

14 Repeat steps 11–13 on the top.

15 Repeat steps 11–14 on the right.

16 Fold and unfold on the left.

17 Repeat step 16 three more times.

18 Fold and unfold along the creases. Unfold at the top and bottom.

19 Push in at the dots and fold along the creases. The model will be 3D.

20 Tuck into the center.

21 Uniform Triangular Prism

Bronze Triangular Prism

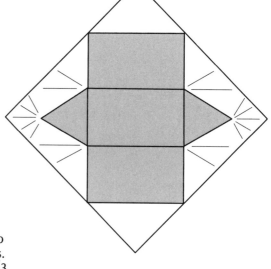

This triangular prism is composed of two equilateral triangles and three rectangles. Each rectangle has dimensions of 1 by √3. Even/odd symmetry is used.

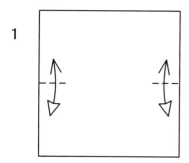

1

Fold and unfold on the edges.

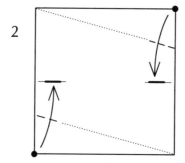

2

Crease at the edges.

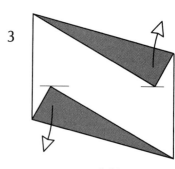

3

Unfold.

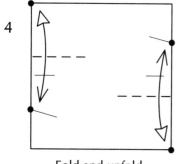

4

Fold and unfold, creasing lightly.

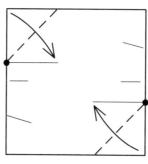

5

Rotate.

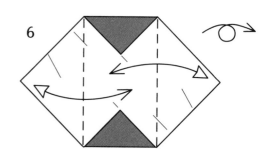

6

Fold and unfold.

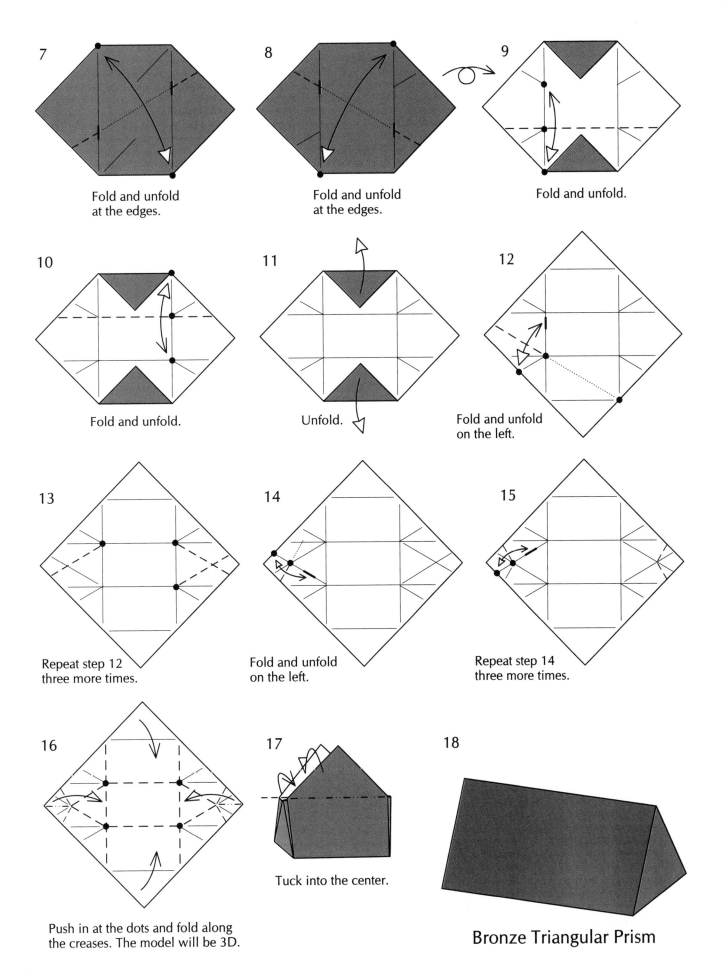

7

Fold and unfold
at the edges.

8

Fold and unfold
at the edges.

9

Fold and unfold.

10

Fold and unfold.

11

Unfold.

12

Fold and unfold
on the left.

13

Repeat step 12
three more times.

14

Fold and unfold
on the left.

15

Repeat step 14
three more times.

16

Push in at the dots and fold along
the creases. The model will be 3D.

17

Tuck into the center.

18

Bronze Triangular Prism

Silver Rectangular Prism

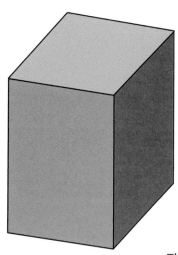

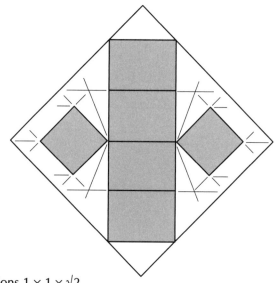

This tall rectangular prism has dimensions $1 \times 1 \times \sqrt{2}$.
It is a variation of the cube.

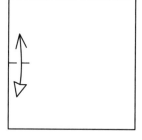

1

Fold and unfold
on the left.

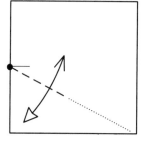

2

Fold and unfold
creasing lightly.

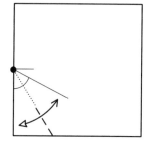

3

Fold and unfold
at the bottom.

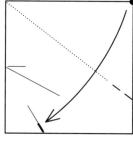

4

Fold the corner
to the crease.

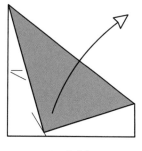

5

Unfold.

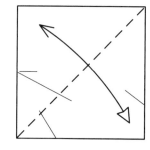

6

Fold and unfold.

7

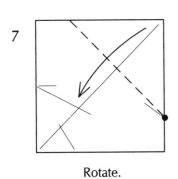

Rotate.

8

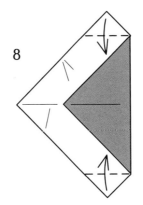

9

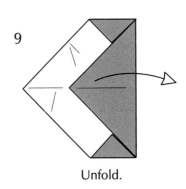

Unfold.

10

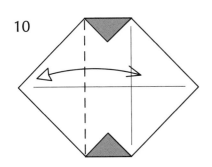

Fold and unfold.

11

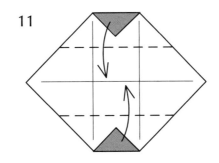

12

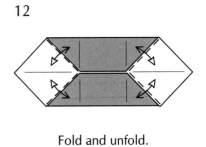

Fold and unfold.

13

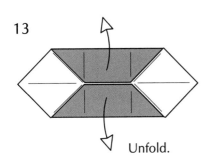

Unfold.

15

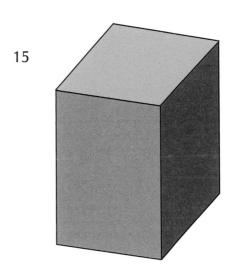

Silver Rectangular Prism

14

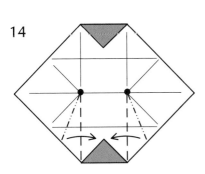

Continue with steps 10 through the end of the Cube (page 82).

Tall Rectangular Prism

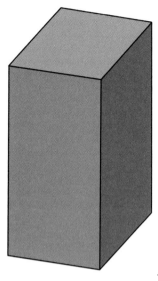

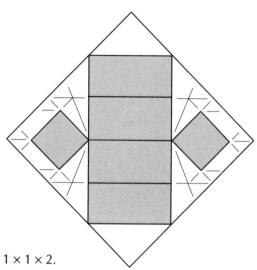

This tall rectangular prism has dimensions $1 \times 1 \times 2$.
This is similar to the silver rectangular prism.

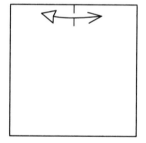

1

Fold and unfold at the top.

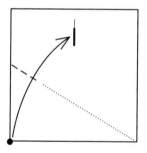

2

Crease on the left.

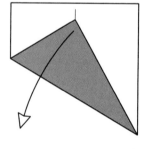

3

Unfold.

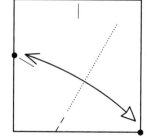

4

Fold and unfold at the bottom.

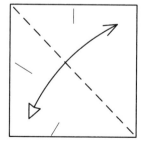

5

Fold and unfold in the center.

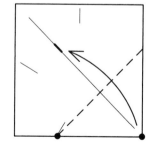

6

7

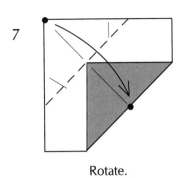

Rotate.

8

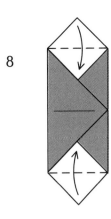

9

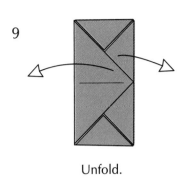

Unfold.

10

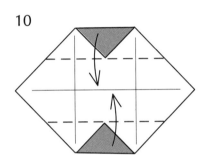

11

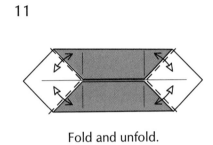

Fold and unfold.

12

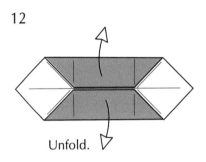

Unfold.

13

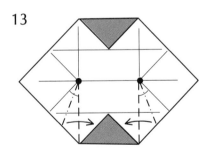

Continue with steps 10 through the end of the Cube (page 82).

14

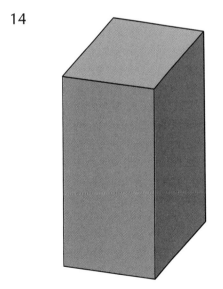

Tall Rectangular Prism

Rectangular Prism with Triangles

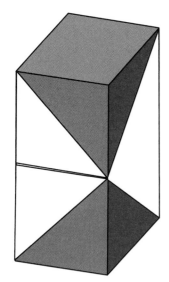

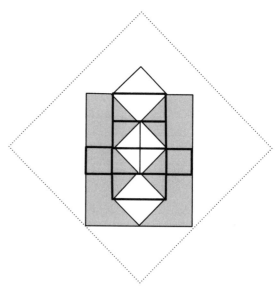

This rectangular prism has dimensions 1 × 1 × 2. The crease pattern shows step 13, and the shape inside the bold lines are the sides of the prism. The paper is divided into fifths. Even symmetry is used.

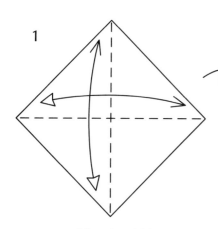

1

Fold and unfold.

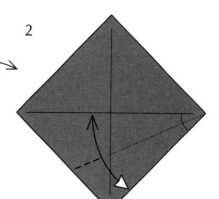

2

Fold and unfold on the left.

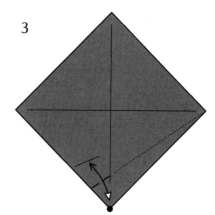

3

Fold to the crease and unfold.

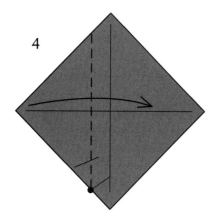

4

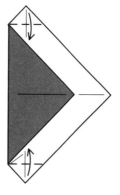

5

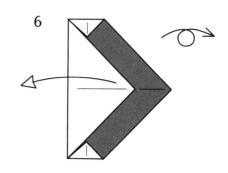

6

Unfold and rotate.

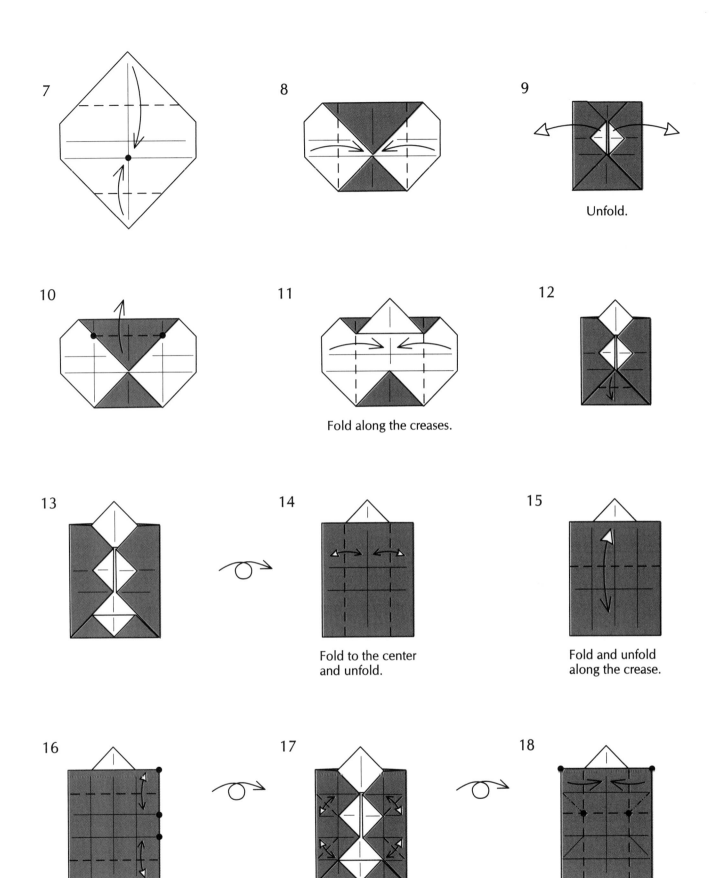

7

8

9

Unfold.

10

11

Fold along the creases.

12

13

14

Fold to the center
and unfold.

15

Fold and unfold
along the crease.

16

Fold and unfold.

17

Fold and unfold.

18

Push in at the lower dots.
The upper dots will meet.

19

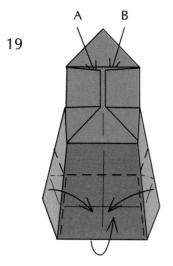

Note the pockets A and B.
Repeat step 18 at the front.

20

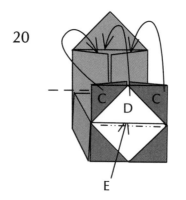

Tuck C into pocket A and tuck
D into B. Note pocket E.

21

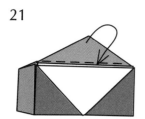

Tuck into pocket E.
Rotate.

22

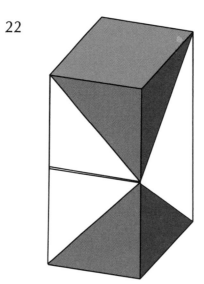

**Rectangular Prism
with Triangles**

Striped Rectangular Prism

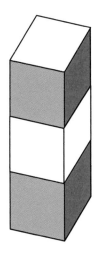

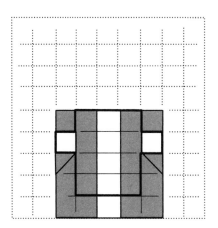

This rectangular prism has dimensions 1 × 1 × 3. The height is 1/3 the length of the side of the square paper. The square is divided into 9ths. The crease pattern shows the back of step 18, and the shape inside the bold lines are the sides of the prism. This model has even symmetry.

1

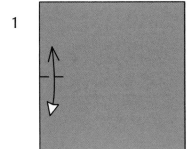

Fold and unfold
on the left.

2

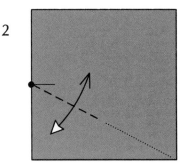

Fold and unfold
on the left.

3

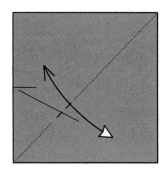

Fold and unfold at
the intersection.

4

├─1/3─┤

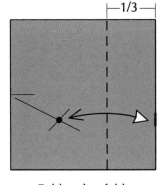

Fold and unfold.

5

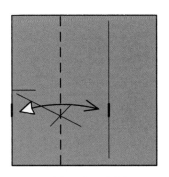

Fold and unfold.

6

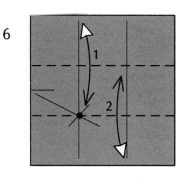

Fold and unfold.

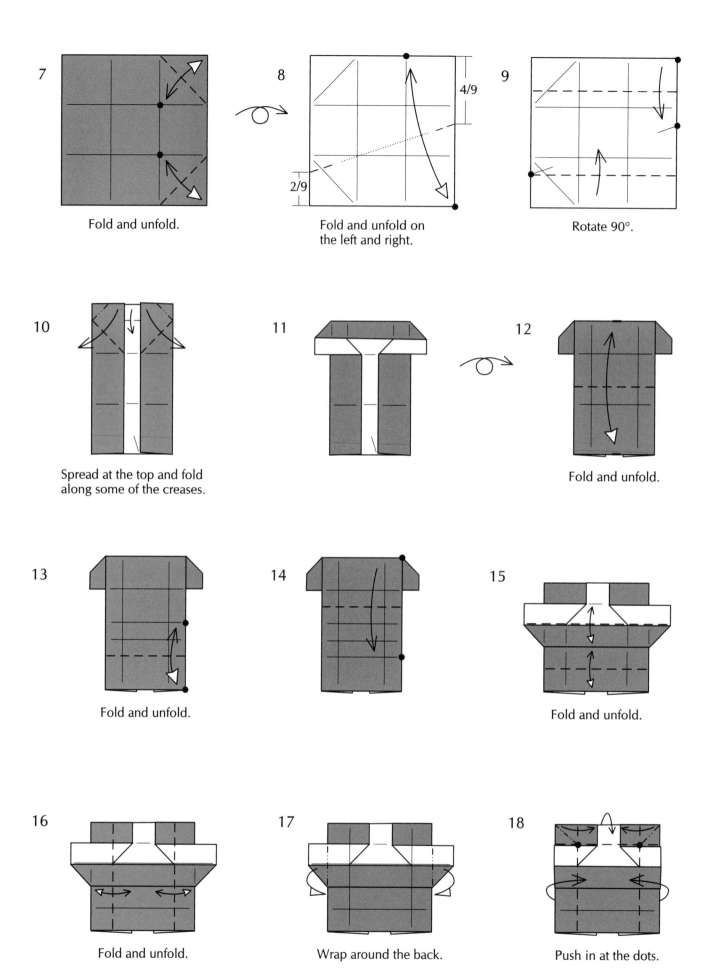

7

Fold and unfold.

8

4/9

2/9

Fold and unfold on
the left and right.

9

Rotate 90°.

10

Spread at the top and fold
along some of the creases.

11

12

Fold and unfold.

13

Fold and unfold.

14

15

Fold and unfold.

16

Fold and unfold.

17

Wrap around the back.

18

Push in at the dots.

19

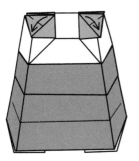

The model is 3D.

20

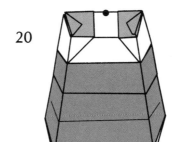

Rotate the dot to the front.

21

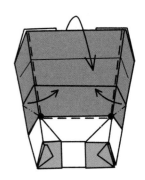

Push in at the dots.

22

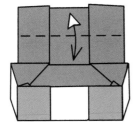

Fold and unfold.

23

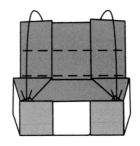

Tuck inside and rotate.

24

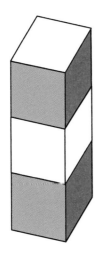

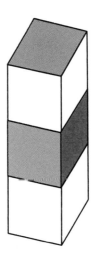

Striped Rectangular Prisms

Uniform Pentagonal Prism

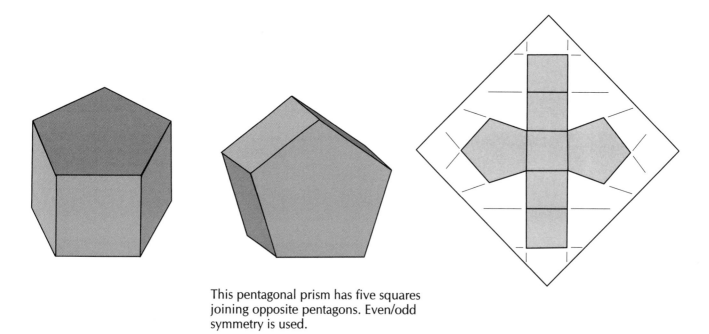

This pentagonal prism has five squares joining opposite pentagons. Even/odd symmetry is used.

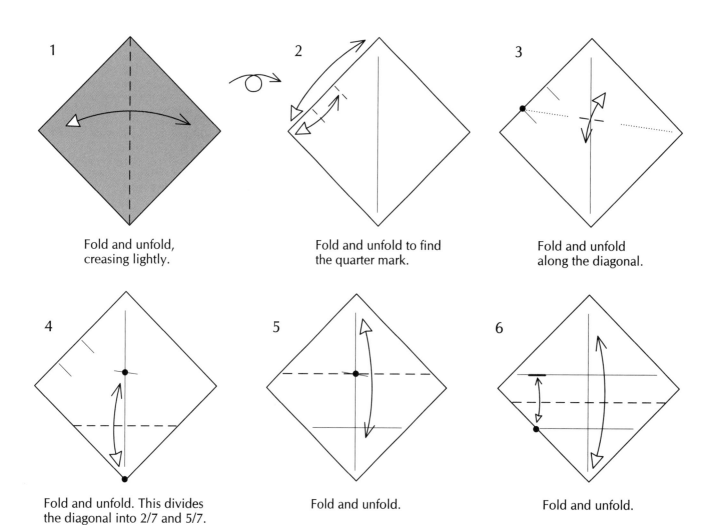

1 Fold and unfold, creasing lightly.

2 Fold and unfold to find the quarter mark.

3 Fold and unfold along the diagonal.

4 Fold and unfold. This divides the diagonal into 2/7 and 5/7.

5 Fold and unfold.

6 Fold and unfold.

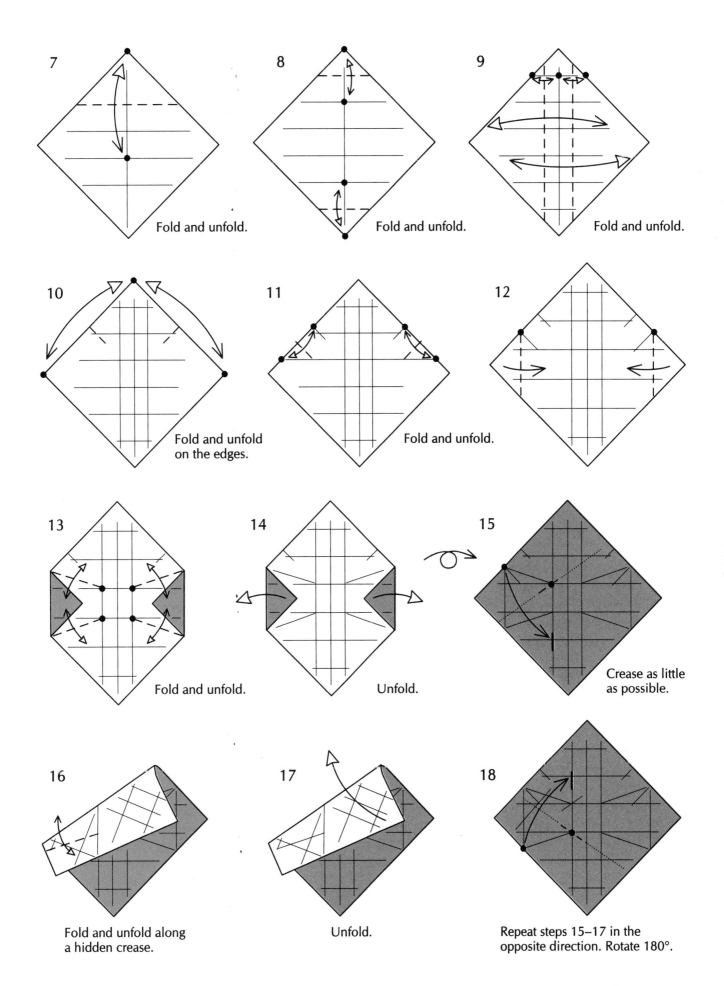

7 Fold and unfold.

8 Fold and unfold.

9 Fold and unfold.

10 Fold and unfold on the edges.

11 Fold and unfold.

12

13 Fold and unfold.

14 Unfold.

15 Crease as little as possible.

16 Fold and unfold along a hidden crease.

17 Unfold.

18 Repeat steps 15–17 in the opposite direction. Rotate 180°.

19

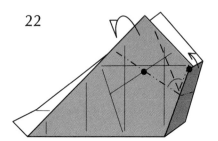

Repeat steps 15–18.

20

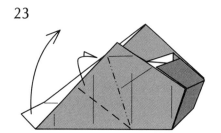

Fold along the crease.

21

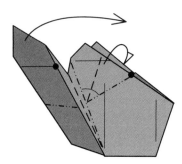

Push in at the dots. Bisect the angles. Rotate to view the side.

22

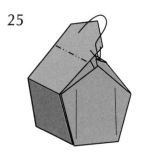

The dots will meet. Flatten inside and repeat behind.

23

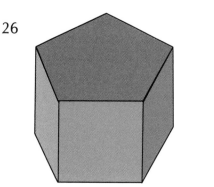

Repeat behind.

24

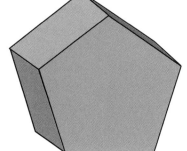

Bisect and flatten inside. The dots will meet. Repeat behind.

25

Tuck the tab inside the pocket.

26

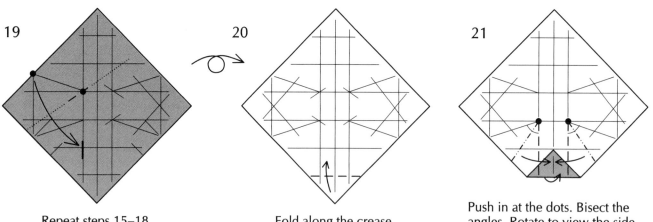

Uniform Pentagonal Prism

Uniform Hexagonal Prism

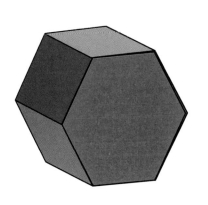

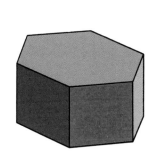

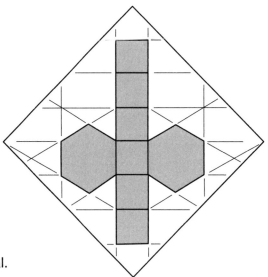

This hexagonal prism is composed of two hexagons and six squares. The paper is divided into eighths along the diagonal. The crease pattern shows even symmetry.

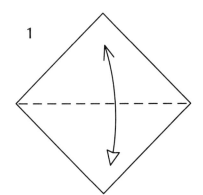

1

Fold and unfold.

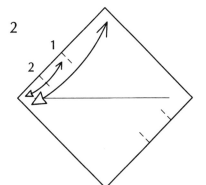

2

Fold and unfold to divide into fourths.

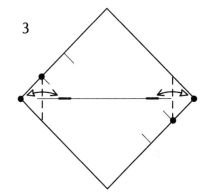

3

Fold and unfold.

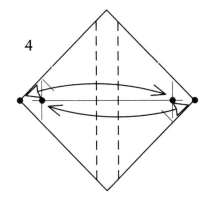

4

Fold and unfold.

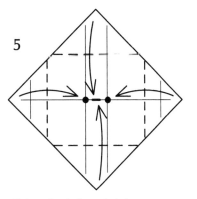

5

Bring the left and right corners to the dots. Bring the top and bottom corners to the center.

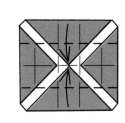

6

Fold to the center.

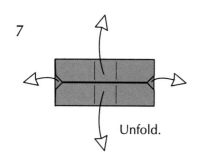

7

Unfold.

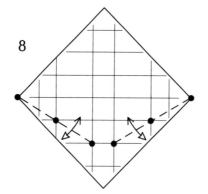

8

Fold and unfold.

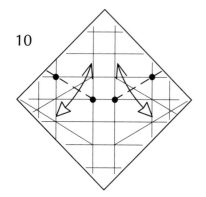

9

Fold and unfold.

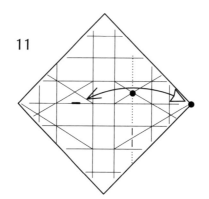

10

Fold and unfold.

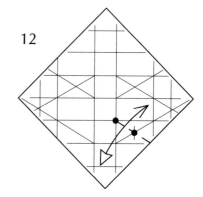

11

Fold and unfold by
the intersection.

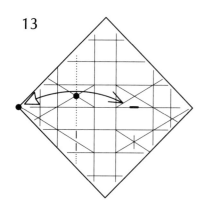

12

Fold and unfold.

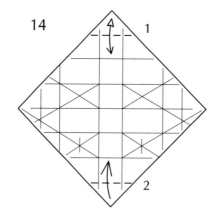

13

Repeat steps
11–12 on the left.

14

1. Fold and unfold along
   the crease.
2. Fold along the crease.

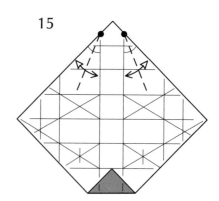

15

Fold and unfold to
bisect the angles.

16

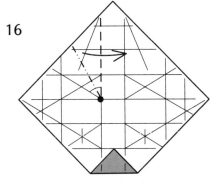

Push in at the dot
and bisect the angle.

17

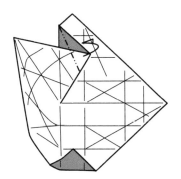

Fold along a partially
hidden crease.

18

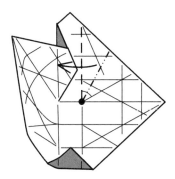

Repeat steps 16–17
on the right.

19

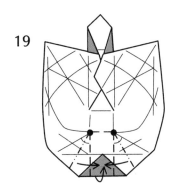

Push in at the dots and bisect the
angles. Rotate to view the side.

20

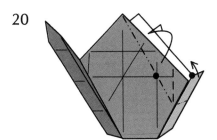

The dots will meet.
Repeat behind.

21

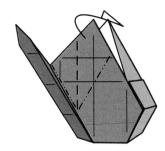

Repeat behind.

22

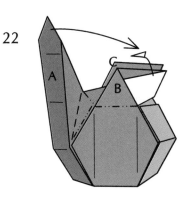

Region A will cover B and C. The
dots will meet. Repeat behind.

23

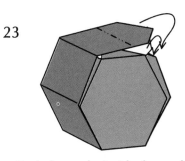

Tuck three tabs inside the pocket.

24

Uniform Hexagonal Prism

Antiprisms

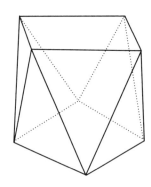

An antiprism is a polyhedron where two congruent polygons are connected by a band of alternating triangles. For a uniform antiprism, the triangles are equilateral triangles.

Here is a collection of antiprisms, including the octahedron from the Platonic Solids section.

Uniform Antiprisms.

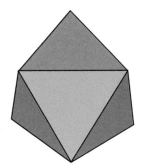

Uniform Triangular Antiprism (Octahedron)

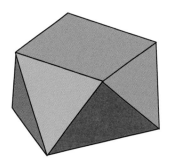

Uniform Square Antiprism

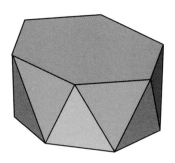

Uniform Hexagonal Antiprism

More Antiprisms.

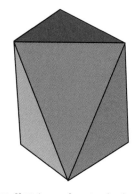

Tall Triangular Antiprism

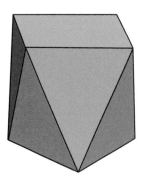

Tall Square Antiprism

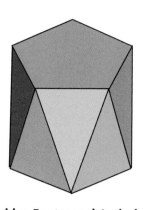

Golden Pentagonal Antiprism

Tall Triangular Antiprism

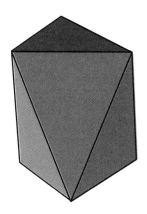

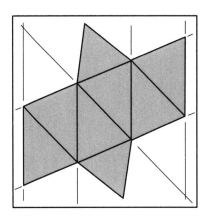

A triangular antiprism is composed of six isosceles triangles and two equilateral triangles. In this one, the angles of the isosceles triangles are 45°, 67.5°, and 67.5°. The triangles form a band wrapping around. The crease pattern shows odd symmetry since it is the same when rotated 180°.

1

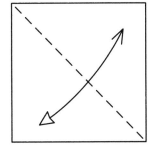

Fold and unfold.

2

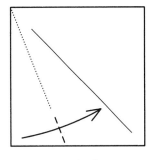

Crease at the bottom.

3

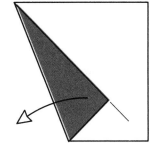

Unfold.

4

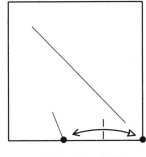

Fold and unfold
at the bottom.

5

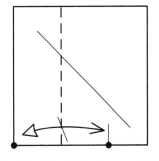

Fold and unfold. Rotate 180°.

6

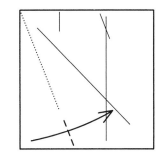

Repeat steps 2–5.

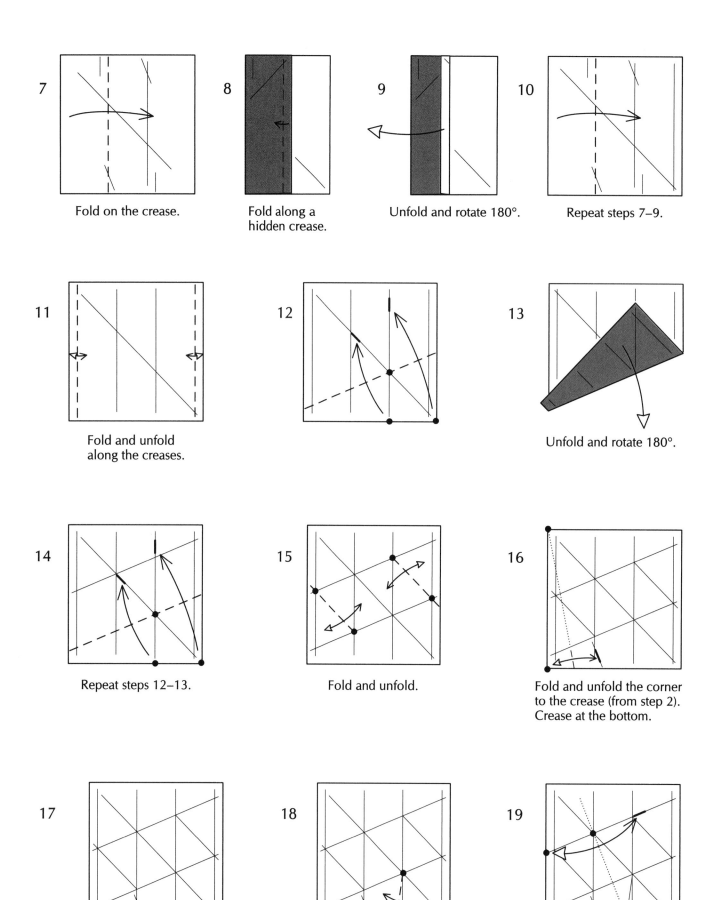

7 Fold on the crease.

8 Fold along a hidden crease.

9 Unfold and rotate 180°.

10 Repeat steps 7–9.

11 Fold and unfold along the creases.

12

13 Unfold and rotate 180°.

14 Repeat steps 12–13.

15 Fold and unfold.

16 Fold and unfold the corner to the crease (from step 2). Crease at the bottom.

17 Fold and unfold at the bottom.

18 Fold and unfold.

19 Fold and unfold at the bottom.

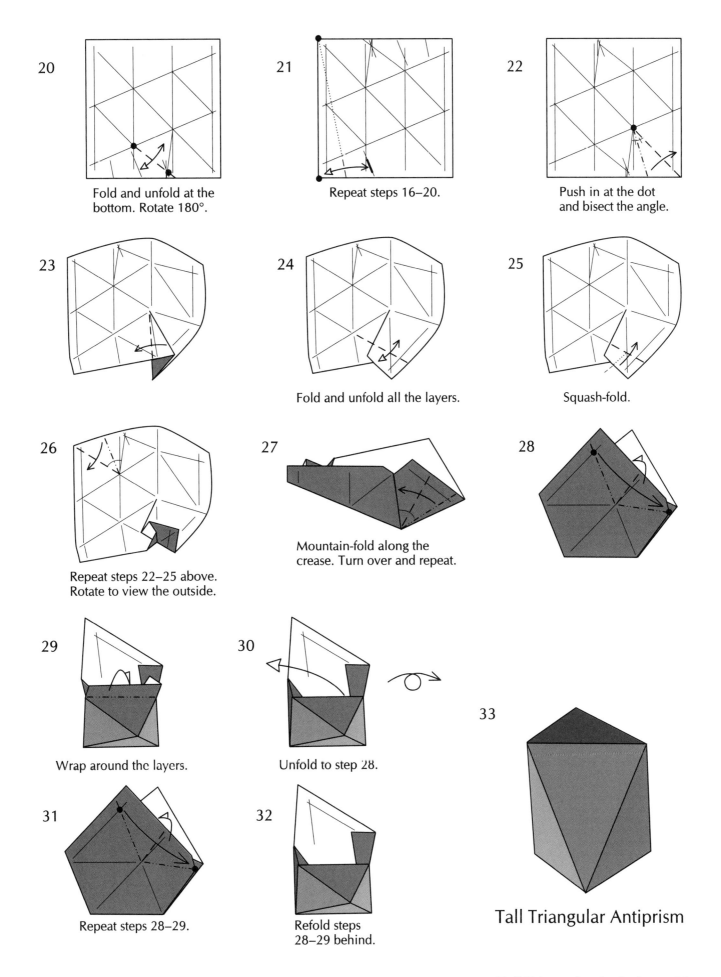

20 Fold and unfold at the bottom. Rotate 180°.

21 Repeat steps 16–20.

22 Push in at the dot and bisect the angle.

23

24 Fold and unfold all the layers.

25 Squash-fold.

26 Repeat steps 22–25 above. Rotate to view the outside.

27 Mountain-fold along the crease. Turn over and repeat.

28

29 Wrap around the layers.

30 Unfold to step 28.

31 Repeat steps 28–29.

32 Refold steps 28–29 behind.

33

Tall Triangular Antiprism

Uniform Square Antiprism

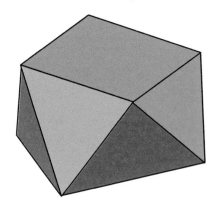

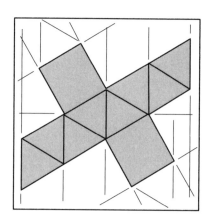

This uniform antiprism is composed of two squares and eight equilateral triangles. The crease pattern shows odd symmetry.

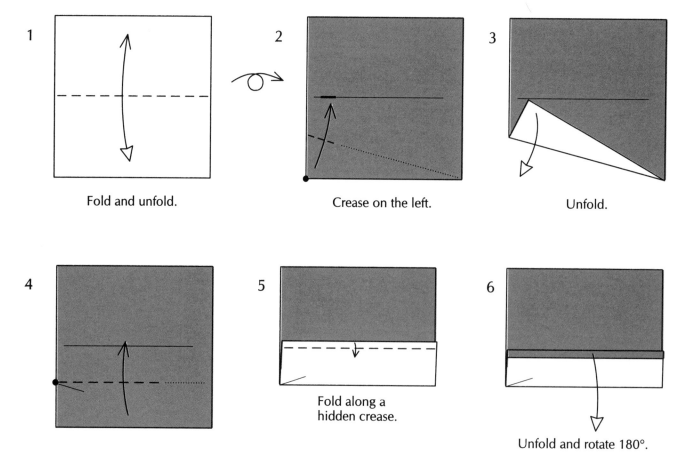

1 Fold and unfold.

2 Crease on the left.

3 Unfold.

4

5 Fold along a hidden crease.

6 Unfold and rotate 180°.

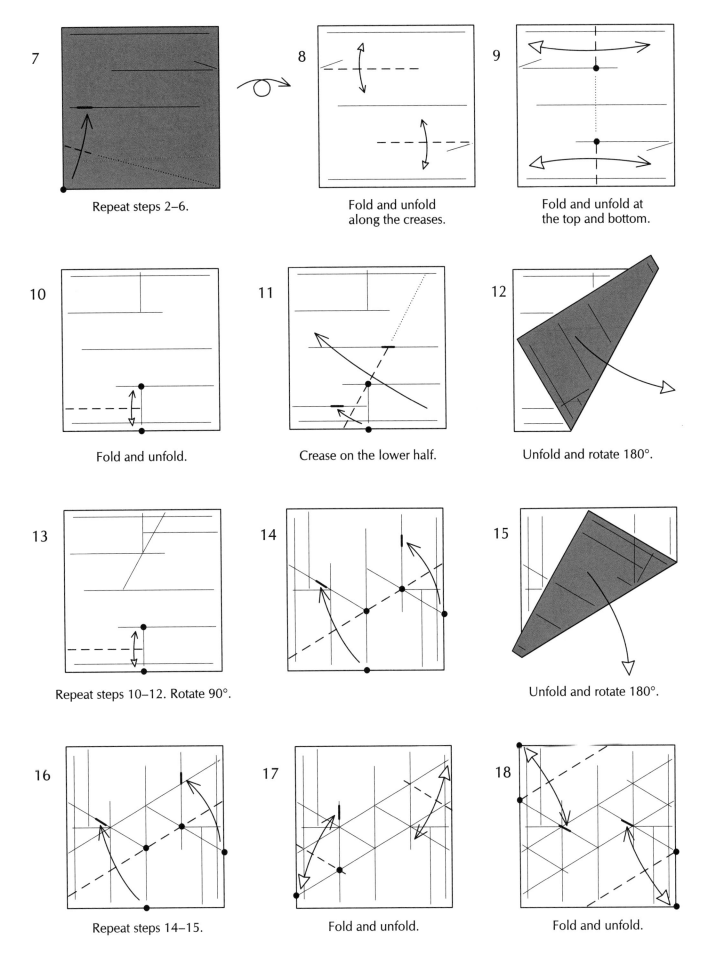

7 Repeat steps 2–6.

8 Fold and unfold along the creases.

9 Fold and unfold at the top and bottom.

10 Fold and unfold.

11 Crease on the lower half.

12 Unfold and rotate 180°.

13 Repeat steps 10–12. Rotate 90°.

14

15 Unfold and rotate 180°.

16 Repeat steps 14–15.

17 Fold and unfold.

18 Fold and unfold.

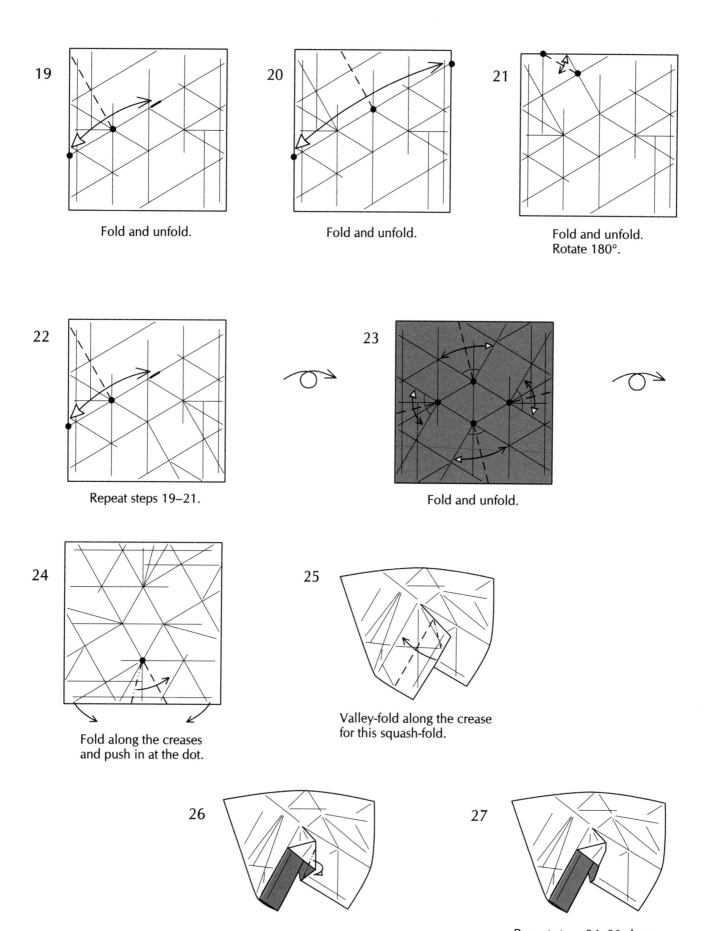

19   Fold and unfold.

20   Fold and unfold.

21   Fold and unfold.
Rotate 180°.

22   Repeat steps 19–21.

23   Fold and unfold.

24   Fold along the creases
and push in at the dot.

25   Valley-fold along the crease
for this squash-fold.

26

27   Repeat steps 24–26 above.
Rotate to view the outside.

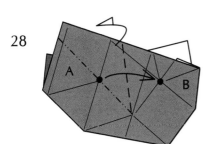

28

Fold along the creases.
Turn over and repeat.

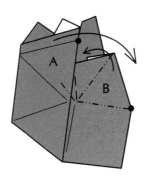

29

Region A will cover B
and the dots will meet.

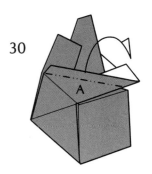

30

Tuck inside by wrapping
around the layers.

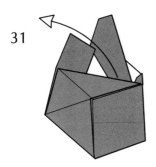

31

Unfold to step 29.

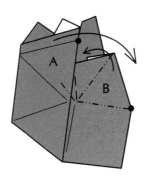

32

Repeat steps 29–30.

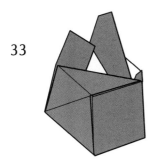

33

Refold steps 29–30 behind.

34

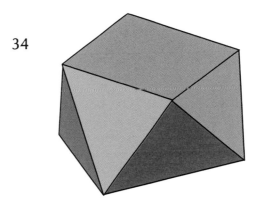

Uniform Square Antiprism

Tall Square Antiprism

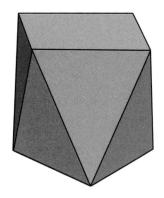

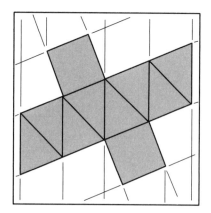

This antiprism is composed of two squares and eight triangles. The triangles are isosceles with angles 45°, 67.5°, and 67.5°. Odd symmetry is used.

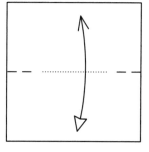

1

Fold and unfold
on the edges.

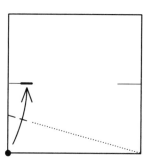

2

Fold on the left.

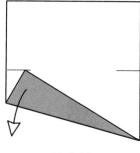

3

Unfold.

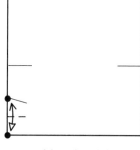

4

Fold and unfold
on the left.

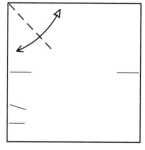

5

Fold and unfold
at the top.

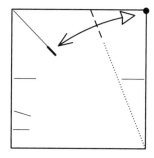

6

Fold and unfold
at the top.

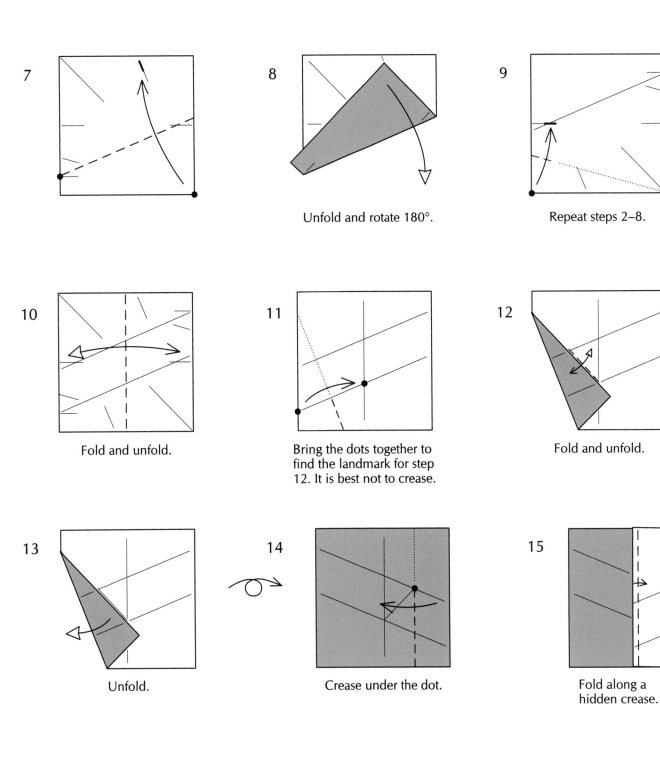

7

8

Unfold and rotate 180°.

9

Repeat steps 2–8.

10

Fold and unfold.

11

Bring the dots together to
find the landmark for step
12. It is best not to crease.

12

Fold and unfold.

13

Unfold.

14

Crease under the dot.

15

Fold along a
hidden crease.

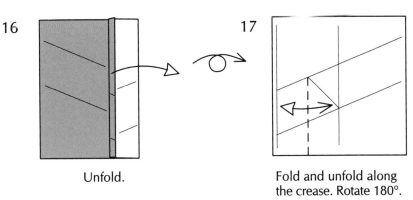

16

Unfold.

17

Fold and unfold along
the crease. Rotate 180°.

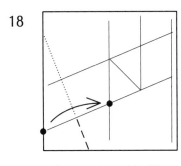

18

Repeat steps 11–17.

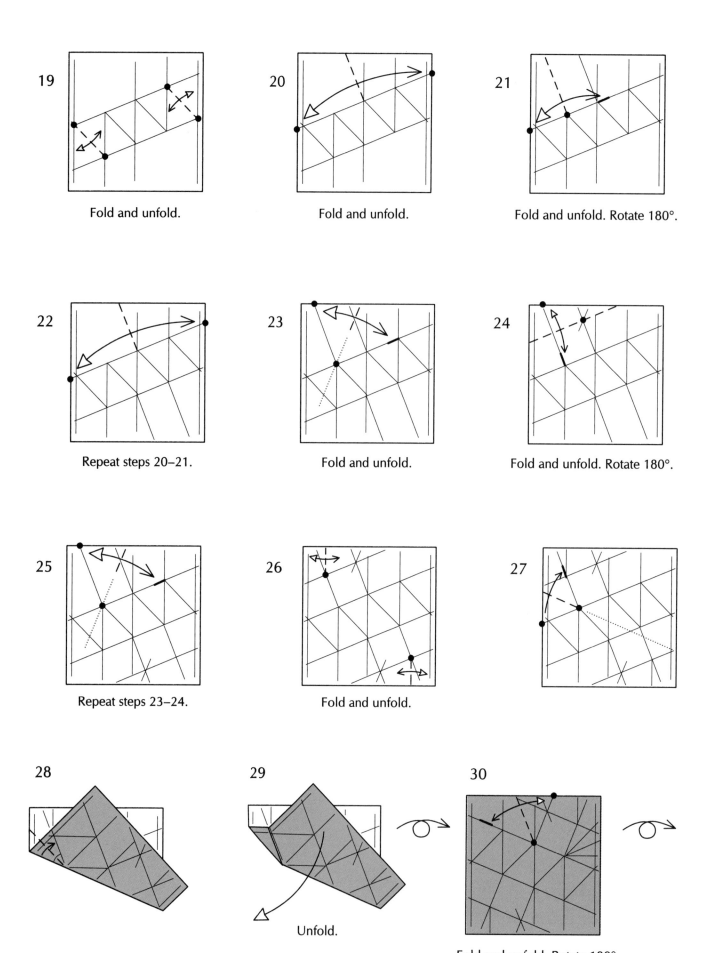

19 Fold and unfold.

20 Fold and unfold.

21 Fold and unfold. Rotate 180°.

22 Repeat steps 20–21.

23 Fold and unfold.

24 Fold and unfold. Rotate 180°.

25 Repeat steps 23–24.

26 Fold and unfold.

27

28

29 Unfold.

30 Fold and unfold. Rotate 180°.

31

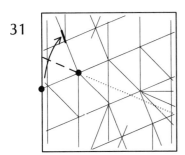

Repeat steps 27–30.

32

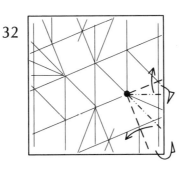

Push in at the dot and fold along the creases.

33

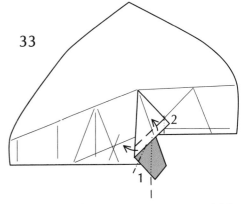

This is a combination of two squash folds.
1. Valley-fold along the hidden crease.
2. Valley-fold along the top crease.

34

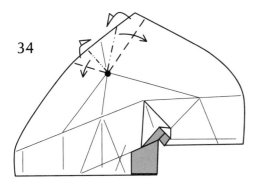

Repeat steps 32–33 above.
Rotate to view the outside.

35

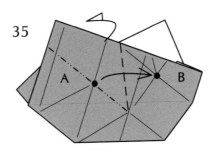

Turn over and repeat.

36

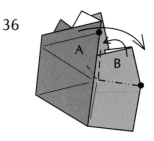

Region A will cover B and the dots will meet.

37

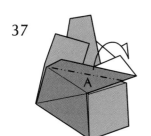

Tuck inside by wrapping around the layers.

38

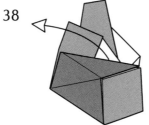

Unfold to step 36.

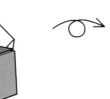

39

Repeat steps 36–37.

40

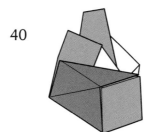

Refold steps 36–37 behind.

41

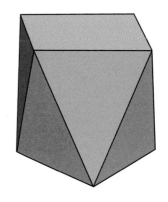

Tall Square Antiprism

Golden Pentagonal Antiprism

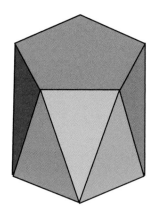

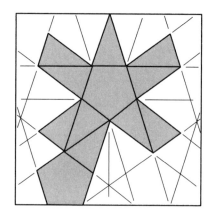

A pentagonal antiprism is composed of ten triangles and two pentagons. In this one, the angles of each triangle are 36°, 72°, and 72°. This uses mainly even symmetry.

1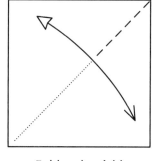

Fold and unfold
by the top.

2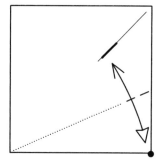

Fold and unfold
on the right.

3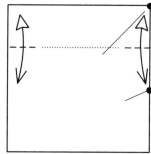

Fold and unfold
on the edges.

4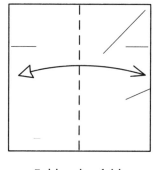

Fold and unfold,
creasing lightly.

5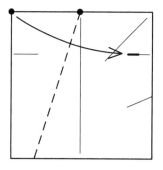

6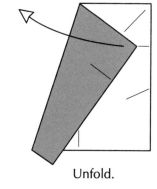

Unfold.

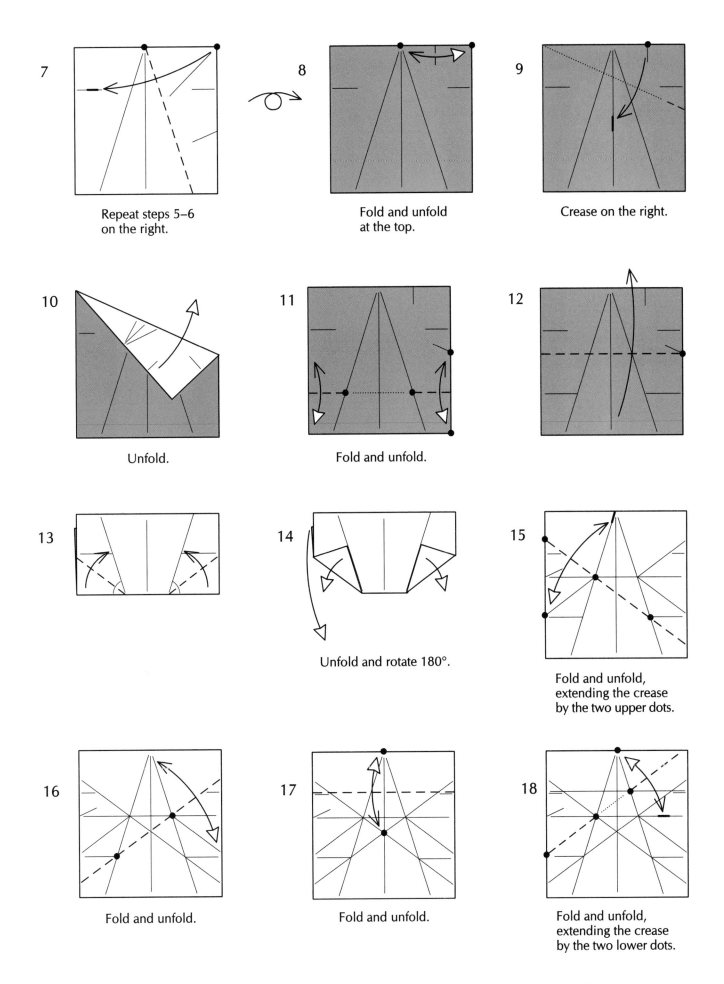

7　Repeat steps 5–6 on the right.

8　Fold and unfold at the top.

9　Crease on the right.

10　Unfold.

11　Fold and unfold.

12

13　Fold and unfold.

14　Unfold and rotate 180°.

15　Fold and unfold, extending the crease by the two upper dots.

16　Fold and unfold.

17　Fold and unfold.

18　Fold and unfold, extending the crease by the two lower dots.

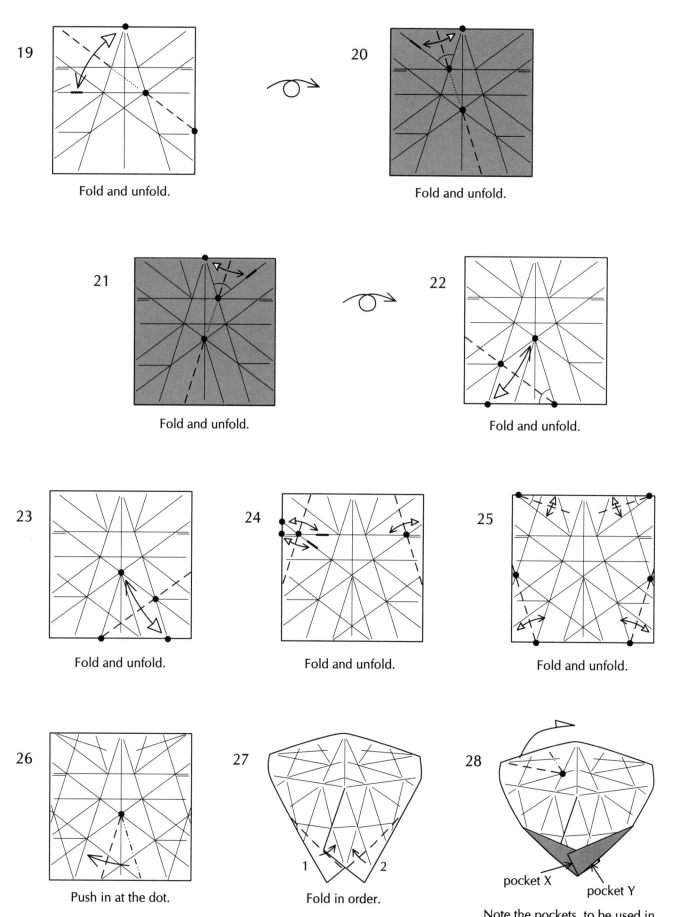

19 Fold and unfold.

20 Fold and unfold.

21 Fold and unfold.

22 Fold and unfold.

23 Fold and unfold.

24 Fold and unfold.

25 Fold and unfold.

26 Push in at the dot.

27 Fold in order.

1   2

28 pocket X   pocket Y

Note the pockets, to be used in steps 33–34. Push in at the dot.

29

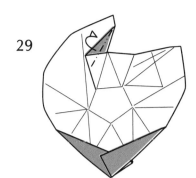

30

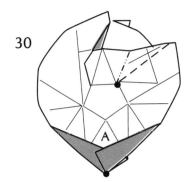

Repeat steps 28–29 on the right.
Rotate to view the outside so the
dot at the bottom goes to the top.

31

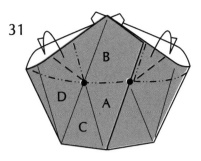

Puff out at the dots and
flatten inside. Rotate
slightly to view the left.

32

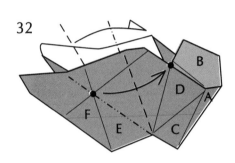

Repeat behind.

33

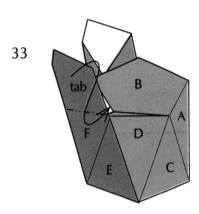

Tuck the tab into pocket X.
(See step 28.)

34

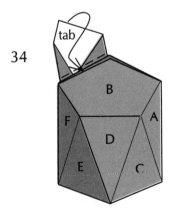

Tuck the tab
into pocket Y.

35

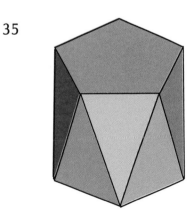

Golden Pentagonal Antiprism

Uniform Hexagonal Antiprism

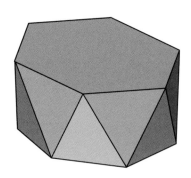

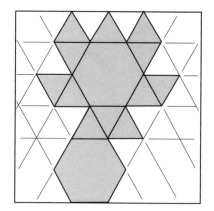

This antiprism is composed of two hexagons and twelve equilateral triangles. The crease pattern shows mainly even symmetry.

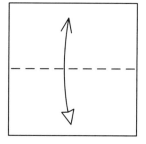

1

Fold and unfold.

2

Fold at the top.

3

Unfold.

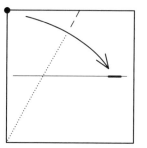

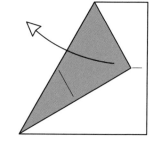

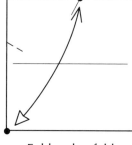

4

Fold and unfold
on the left.

5

6

Unfold.

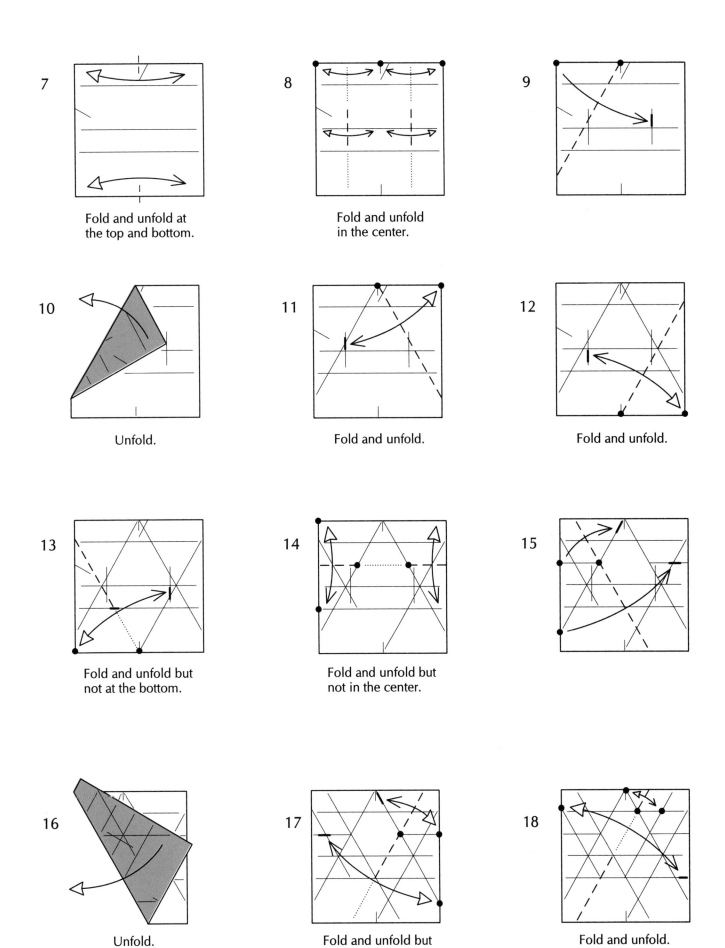

7 Fold and unfold at the top and bottom.

8 Fold and unfold in the center.

9

10 Unfold.

11 Fold and unfold.

12 Fold and unfold.

13 Fold and unfold but not at the bottom.

14 Fold and unfold but not in the center.

15

16 Unfold.

17 Fold and unfold but not at the bottom.

18 Fold and unfold.

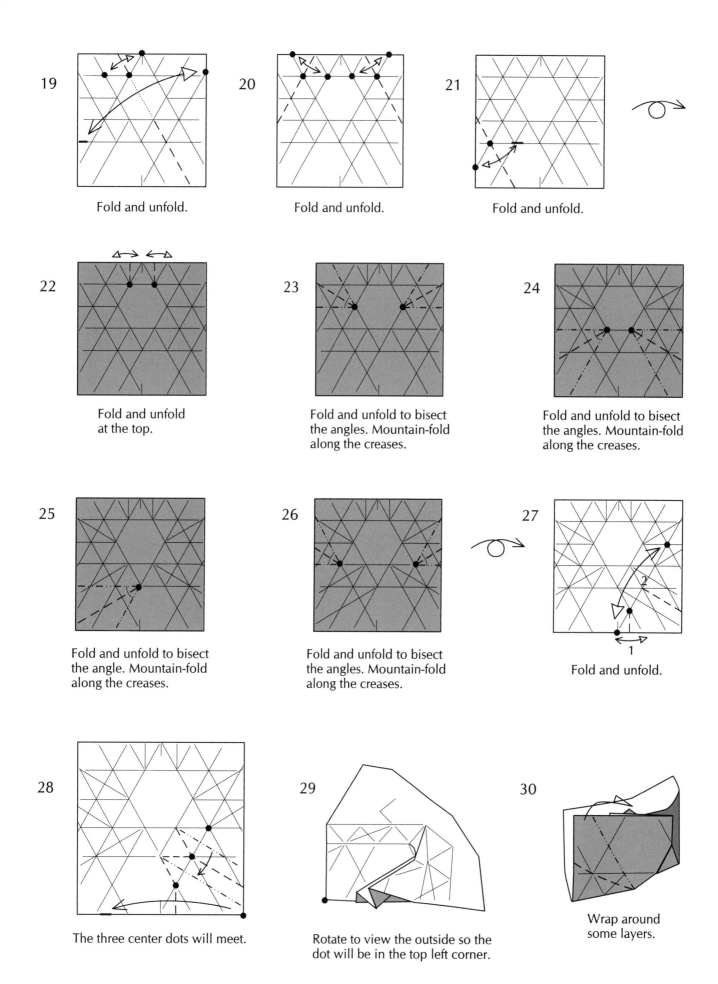

19 Fold and unfold.

20 Fold and unfold.

21 Fold and unfold.

22 Fold and unfold
at the top.

23 Fold and unfold to bisect
the angles. Mountain-fold
along the creases.

24 Fold and unfold to bisect
the angles. Mountain-fold
along the creases.

25 Fold and unfold to bisect
the angle. Mountain-fold
along the creases.

26 Fold and unfold to bisect
the angles. Mountain-fold
along the creases.

27 Fold and unfold.

28 The three center dots will meet.

29 Rotate to view the outside so the
dot will be in the top left corner.

30 Wrap around
some layers.

31

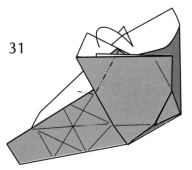

Wrap several layers together.

32

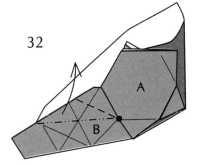

Puff out at the dot.

33

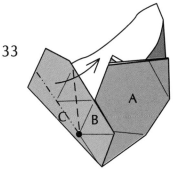

Puff out at the dot. Rotate slightly to view the left.

34

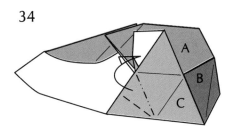

Tuck inside.

35

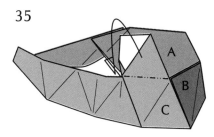

Fold the layers behind.

36

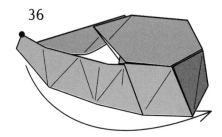

Rotate so the dot goes to the right.

37

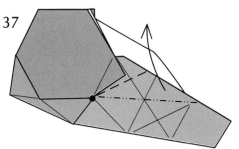

Repeat steps 32–34 in the other direction.

38

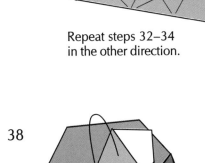

1. Tuck the small tab inside.
2. Tuck the large tab into the pocket. This pocket is hidden from view. It is the opening in the top hexagon.

39

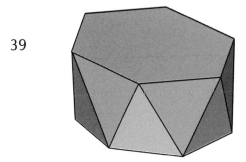

Uniform Hexagonal Antiprism

The Platonic Solids

Platonic Solids.

The five Platonic solids are the tetrahedron, cube, octahedron, icosahedron, and dodecahedron. They are the only polyhedra with the following properties:

1. The faces of each are identical regular polygons.
2. The corners of each are alike.
3. They are convex, meaning line segments connecting any two corners are on or inside the solid.

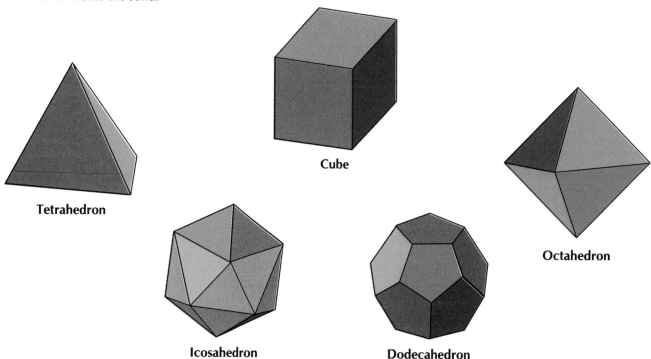

Tetrahedron

Cube

Octahedron

Icosahedron

Dodecahedron

Duals.

Every polyhedron has a dual. The vertices of one polyhedron corresponds to the faces of its dual. For the Platonic Solids, the duals can be found by placing a dot in the center of each face, then connecting the dots as vertices and scaling so both polyhedron and dual are inscribed in the same sphere.

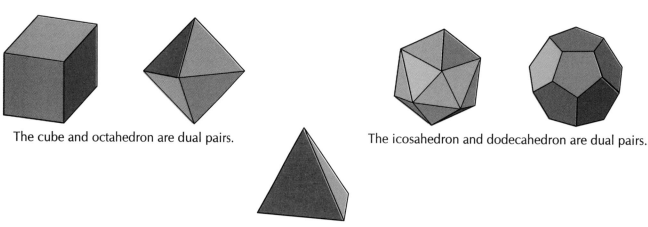

The cube and octahedron are dual pairs.

The icosahedron and dodecahedron are dual pairs.

The tetrahedron is its own dual.

Tetrahedron

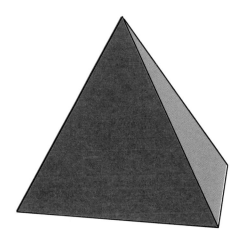

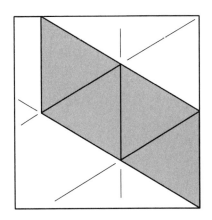

Composed of four equilateral triangles, this is the simplest of the five Platonic solids. Plato believed the tetrahedron represented fire because of its sharpness and simplicity. The crease pattern shows a band of four triangles.

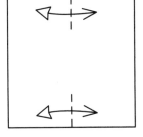

1

Fold and unfold on the top and bottom.

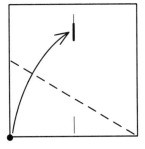

2

Bring the lower corner to the center crease.

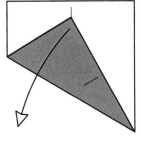

3

Unfold.

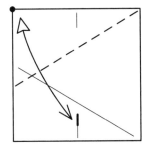

4

Fold and unfold.

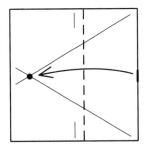

5

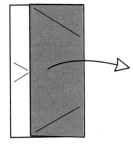

6

Unfold.

7

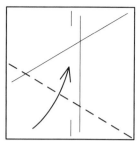

Fold along the crease.

8

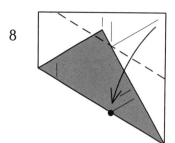

9

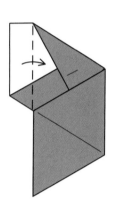

10

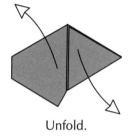

Unfold.

11

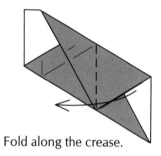

Fold along the crease.

12

13

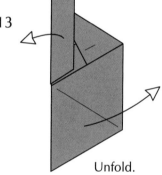

Unfold.

14

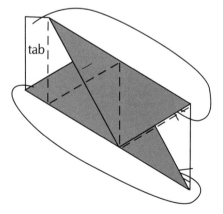

tab

Refold and tuck the tab inside.
Then crease along the edges of
the tetrahedron.

15

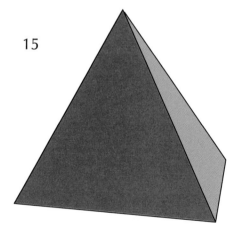

Tetrahedron

Cube

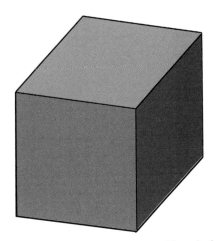

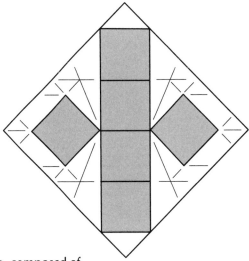

Plato believed this regular polyhedron, composed of six squares, symbolized earth because of its stability.

This cube was designed to be as large as possible from a given size and is larger than the waterbomb cube. The crease patten, using even/odd symmetry, shows a band of four squares.

1

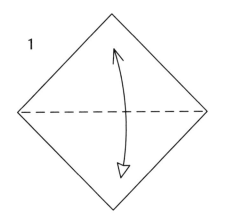

Fold and unfold.

2

Fold and unfold twice to bisect the angles. Crease on the left.

3

4

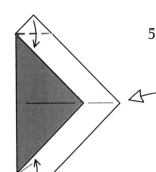

5

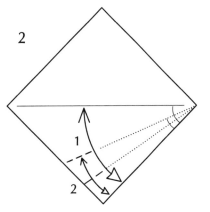

Unfold.

6

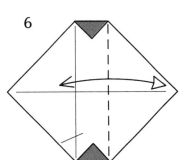

Fold and unfold.

7

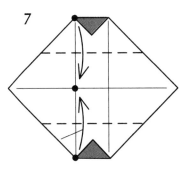

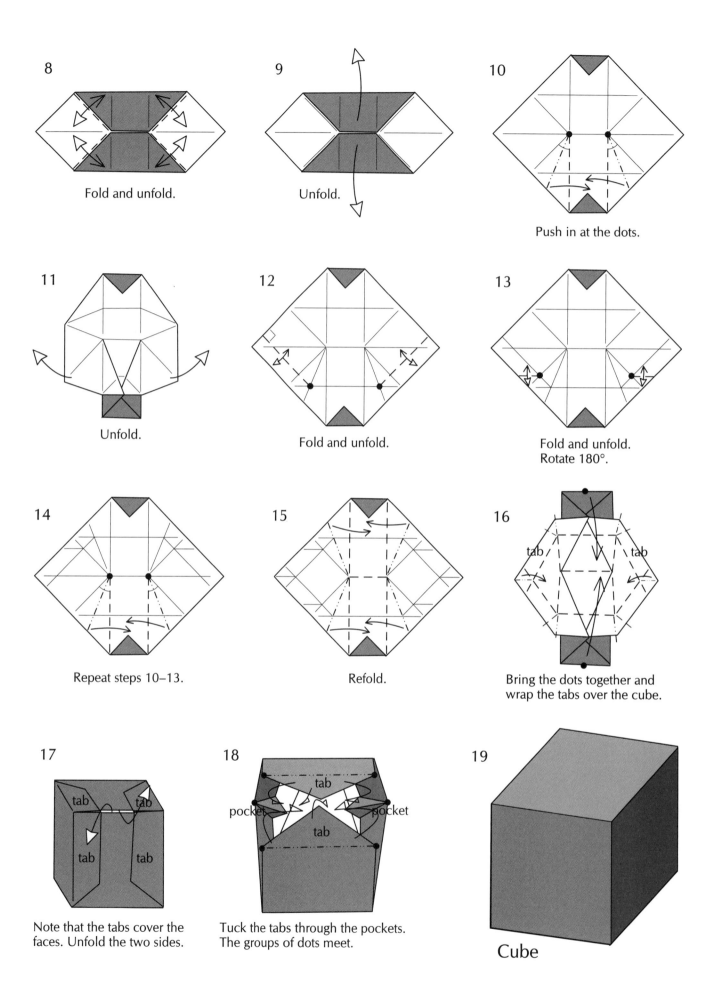

8 Fold and unfold.

9 Unfold.

10 Push in at the dots.

11 Unfold.

12 Fold and unfold.

13 Fold and unfold. Rotate 180°.

14 Repeat steps 10–13.

15 Refold.

16 Bring the dots together and wrap the tabs over the cube.

17 tab tab tab tab

Note that the tabs cover the faces. Unfold the two sides.

18 tab pocket pocket tab

Tuck the tabs through the pockets. The groups of dots meet.

19

Cube

Octahedron

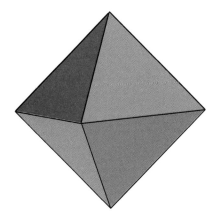

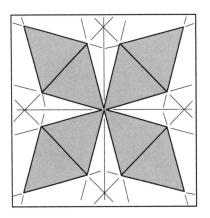

The octahedron is composed of eight equilateral triangles. According to Plato, the octahedron represented air because it appears to be suspended.

The design for this octahedron has square symmetry. Though not my largest octahedron, this one matches in size as the dual to my largest cube (previous model). Both this and the cube are inscribed in a sphere of the same radius. If this octahedron rests on one of the triangular faces, its height is the same as the height of the cube.

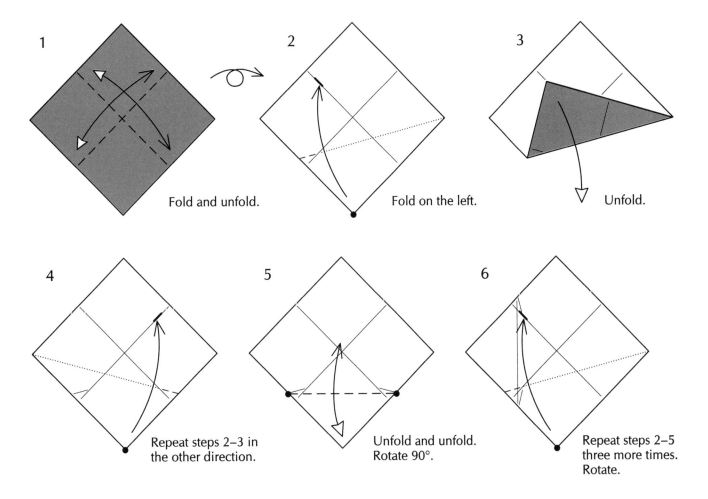

1

Fold and unfold.

2

Fold on the left.

3

Unfold.

4

Repeat steps 2–3 in the other direction.

5

Unfold and unfold.
Rotate 90°.

6

Repeat steps 2–5 three more times.
Rotate.

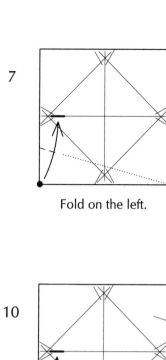

7

Fold on the left.

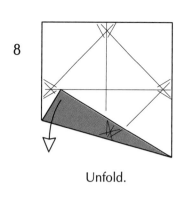

8

Unfold.

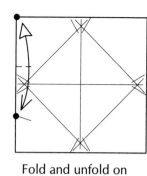

9

Fold and unfold on
the left. Rotate 180°.

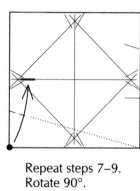

10

Repeat steps 7–9.
Rotate 90°.

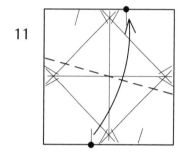

11

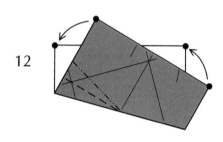

12

Valley-fold along the crease. Turn
over and repeat. The dots will meet.

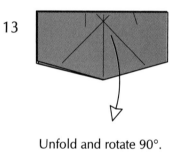

13

Unfold and rotate 90°.

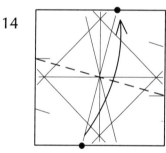

14

Repeat steps 11–13.

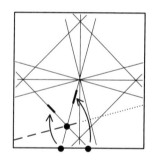

15

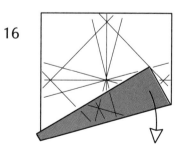

16

Unfold.

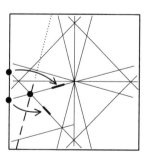

17

Repeat steps 15–16 in the
other direction. Rotate 90°.

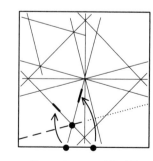

18

Repeat steps 15–17
three more times.

19

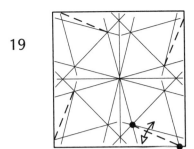

Fold and unfold. Repeat three more times.

20

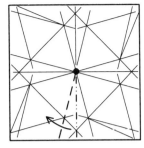

Push in at the dot and fold along the crease.

21

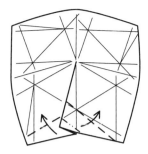

Squash-fold to form a triangle. Valley-fold along the creases.

22

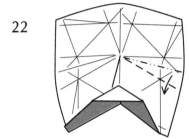

The orientation of the white triangle is not important. Repeat steps 20–21 three more times. Rotate to view the outside.

23

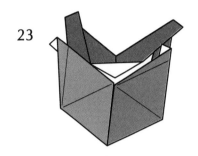

Flatten.

24

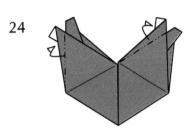

Fold along the creases. Turn over and repeat.

25

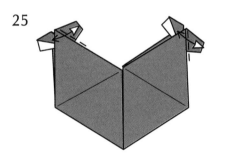

Fold and unfold. Repeat behind.

26

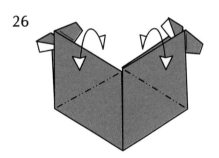

Open to fold inside and unfold. Do not flatten. Repeat behind.

27

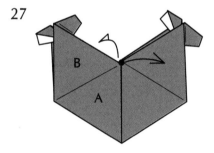

Open and flatten. Follow the dot in the next step.

28

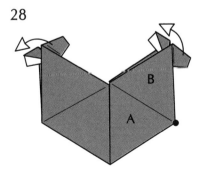

Unfold the thin flaps. Repeat behind.

29

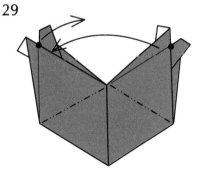

Close the model by interlocking the four tabs. The tabs spiral inward. This method is called a twist lock.

30

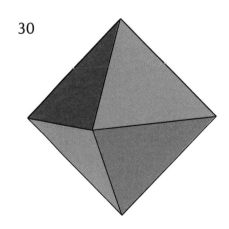

Octahedron

Icosahedron

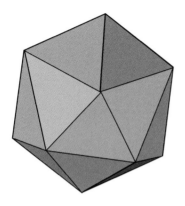

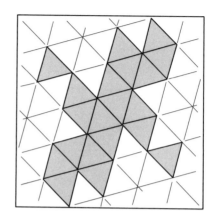

The icosahedron is a regular polyhedron composed of twenty equilateral triangles. Plato attributed this one to water because of its ability to roll. Its dual is the dodecahedron. Odd symmetry is used.

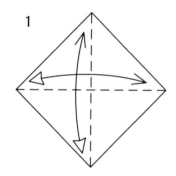

1

Fold and unfold.

2

Fold and unfold at the ends.

3

Fold and unfold on the left.

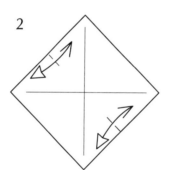

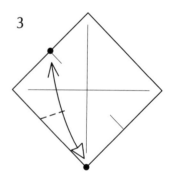

4

Fold and unfold along the diagonal.

5

6

7

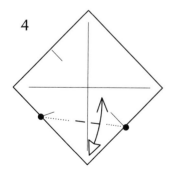

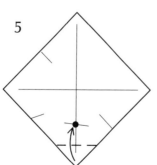

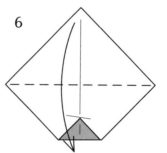

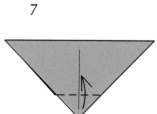

Fold along the hidden edge.

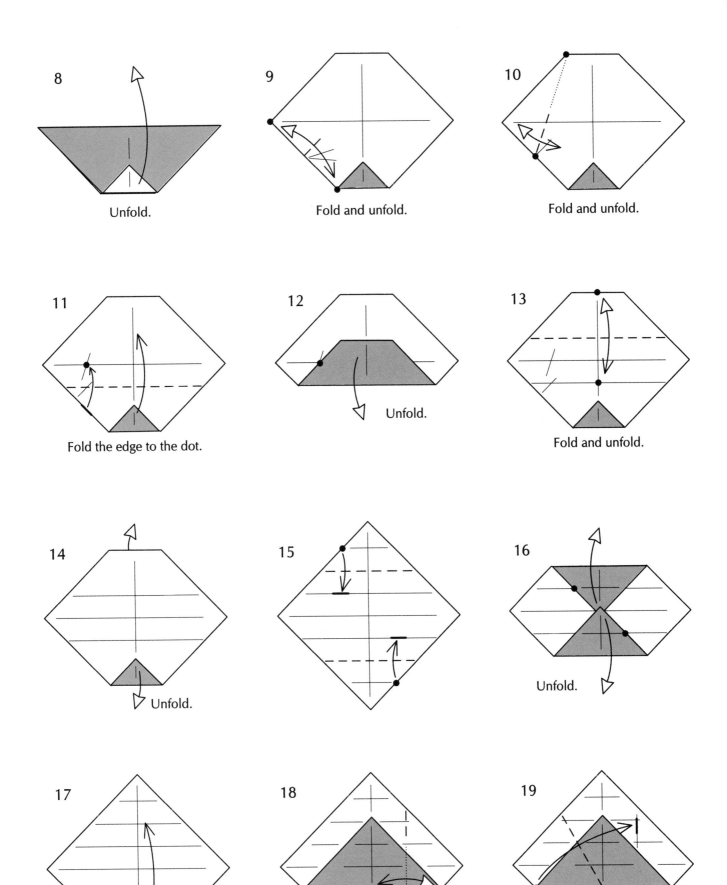

8
Unfold.

9
Fold and unfold.

10
Fold and unfold.

11
Fold the edge to the dot.

12
Unfold.

13
Fold and unfold.

14
Unfold.

15

16
Unfold.

17
Fold along the crease.

18
Fold and unfold near the top.

19

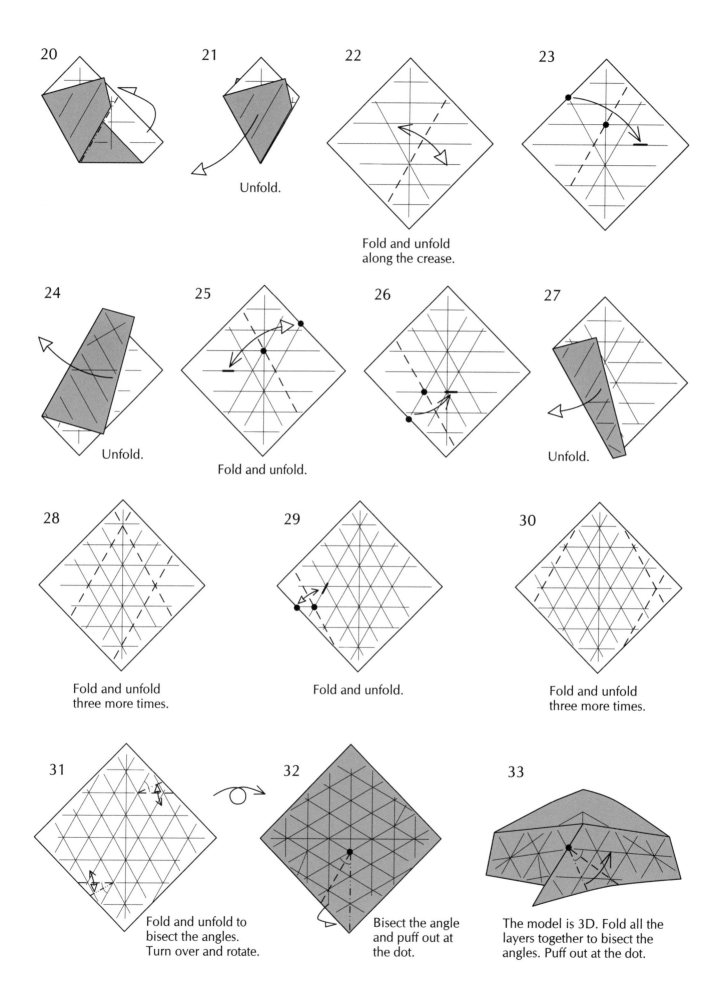

20

21

Unfold.

22

Fold and unfold
along the crease.

23

24

Unfold.

25

Fold and unfold.

26

27

Unfold.

28

Fold and unfold
three more times.

29

Fold and unfold.

30

Fold and unfold
three more times.

31

Fold and unfold to
bisect the angles.
Turn over and rotate.

32

Bisect the angle
and puff out at
the dot.

33

The model is 3D. Fold all the
layers together to bisect the
angles. Puff out at the dot.

34

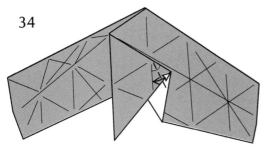

Fold and unfold to
bisect the angle.

35

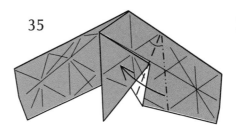

Bisect the angle.

36

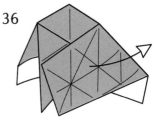

Unfold.

37

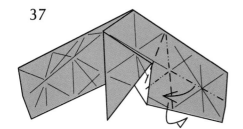

Keep the paper loose.
Fold along the creases.

38

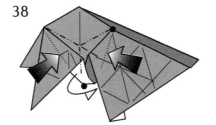

Tuck much of the paper
inside so the lower dot
meets the other one inside.

39

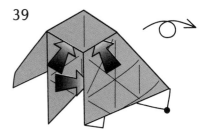

Note the orientation of
the layers. Turn over so
the dot goes to the front.

40

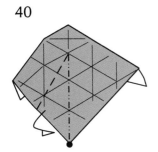

Repeat steps 32–39.

41

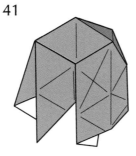

Rotate the top
to the bottom.

42

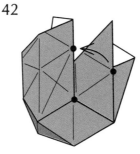

Puff out at the lower dot
while bringing the other
ones together. Fold along
hidden creases from step 34.

43

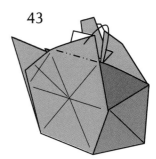

Wrap around
the dark paper.

44

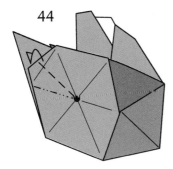

Puff out at the dot and tuck inside
along the creases. The mountain
fold extends inside the model.
Reach inside and press flaps flat
against the inside of the model.

45

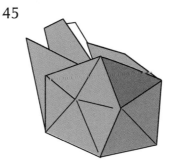

Turn over and repeat
steps 42–44. Adjust the
layers while locking.

46

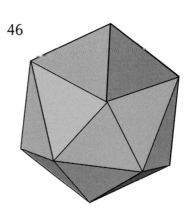

Icosahedron

Dodecahedron

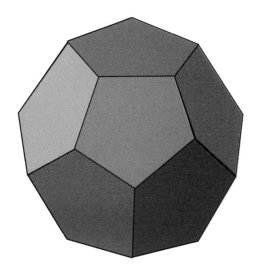

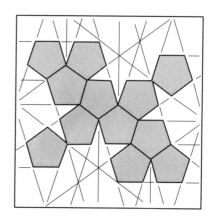

To Plato, this dodecahedron, the quintessence (the "fifth being"), represented the whole universe.

The dodecahedron has twelve pentagonal faces. The crease pattern shows odd symmetry.

1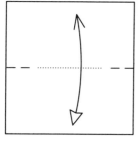

Fold and unfold
on the edges.

2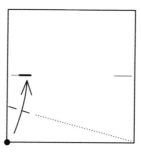

3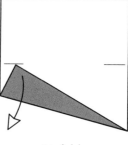

Unfold.

4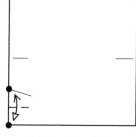

Fold and unfold.
Rotate 180°.

5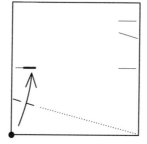

Repeat steps 2–4.

6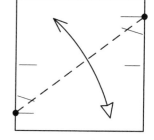

Fold and unfold.

7

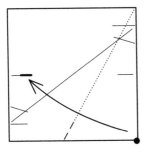

Fold at the bottom.

8

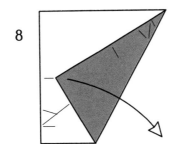

Unfold.

9

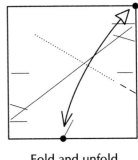

Fold and unfold
on the right.

10

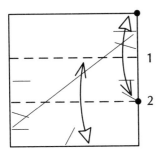

Fold and unfold.

11

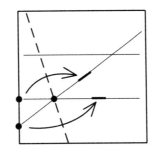

12

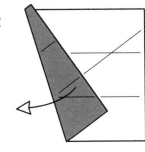

Unfold.

13

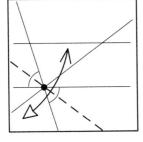

Fold and unfold to
bisect the angle.

14

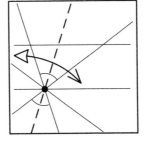

Fold and unfold to bisect
the angle. Rotate 180°.

15

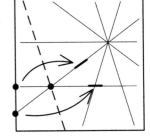

Repeat steps 11–14.

16

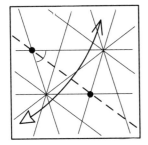

Fold and unfold. Rotate 180°.

17

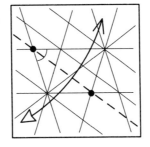

Fold and unfold.

18

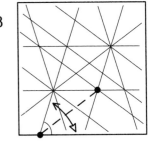

Fold and unfold.

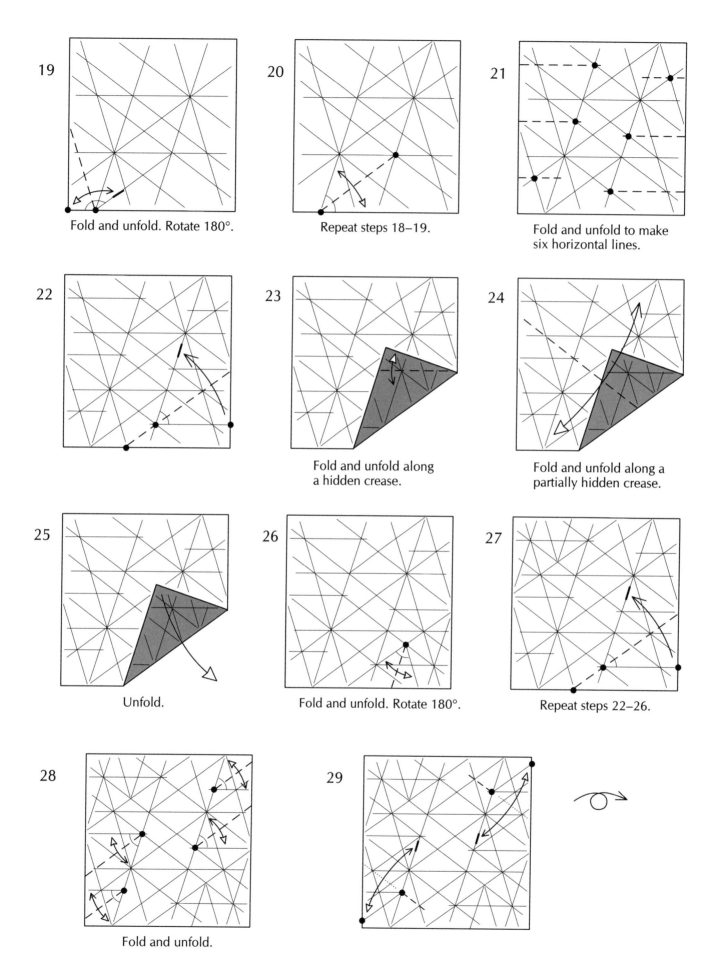

19 Fold and unfold. Rotate 180°.

20 Repeat steps 18–19.

21 Fold and unfold to make six horizontal lines.

23 Fold and unfold along a hidden crease.

24 Fold and unfold along a partially hidden crease.

25 Unfold.

26 Fold and unfold. Rotate 180°.

27 Repeat steps 22–26.

28 Fold and unfold.

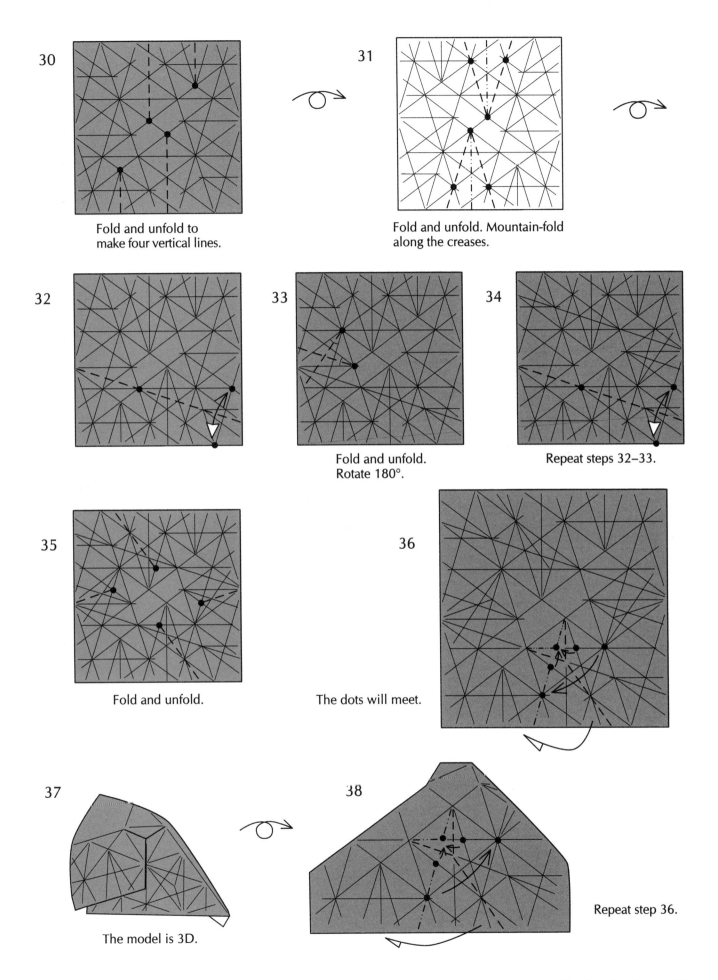

30 Fold and unfold to make four vertical lines.

31 Fold and unfold. Mountain-fold along the creases.

32

33 Fold and unfold. Rotate 180°.

34 Repeat steps 32–33.

35 Fold and unfold.

36 The dots will meet.

37 The model is 3D.

38 Repeat step 36.

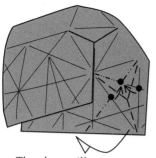

39

The dots will meet.
Turn over and repeat.

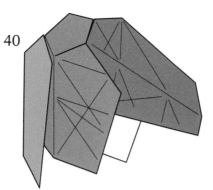

40

Rotate the top to the bottom.

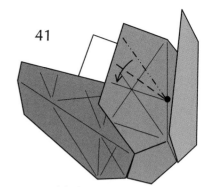

41

Fold along the creases
and puff out at the dot.

42

Fold along the creases
and flatten inside.

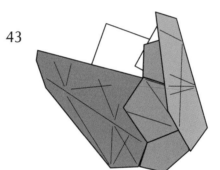

43

Rotate the front to the back.

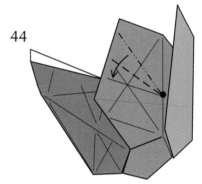

44

Repeat steps 41–42.

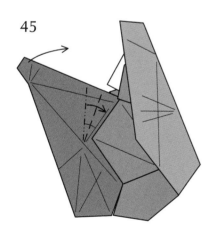

45

Mountain-fold
along the crease.

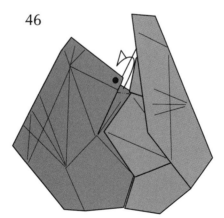

46

Squash-fold behind the dot.

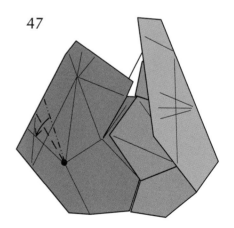

47

Fold along the creases
and puff out at the dot.

48

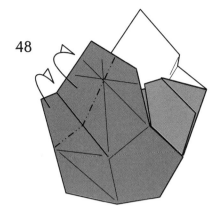

Fold inside and flatten.

49

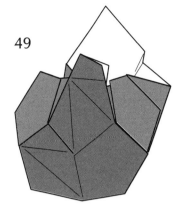

Rotate the front to the back.

50

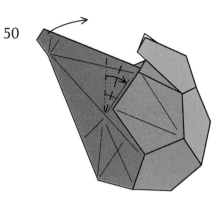

Repeat steps 45–48.

51

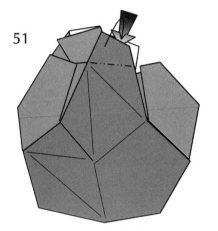

Reverse-fold.

52

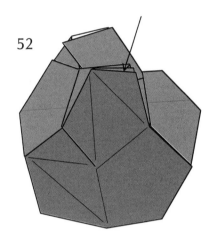

Note the pocket. Rotate the front to the back.

53

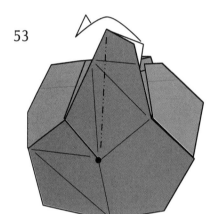

Mountain-fold the partially hidden layer.

54

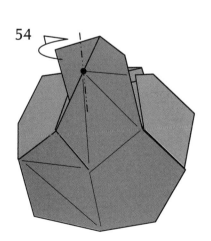

55

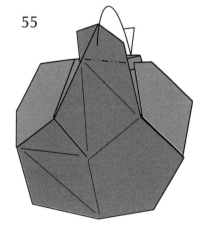

Tuck inside the pocket.

56

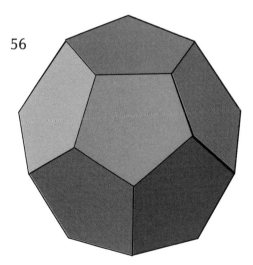

Dodecahedron

Archimedean and Catalan Solids

Archimedean Solids.

The Archimedean polyhedra are convex solids that are made from two or more types of regular polygons and have identical vertices. Here are three of the thirteen Archimedean solids.

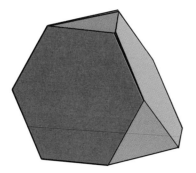

Truncated Tetrahedron

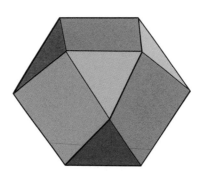

Cuboctahedron

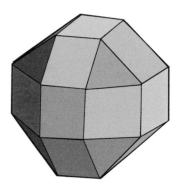

Rhombicuboctahedron

Catalan Solids.

The duals of the Archimedean solids are the Catalan solids. The faces of each solid are identical but not regular polygons. Here are some Catalan solids with a dimpled version.

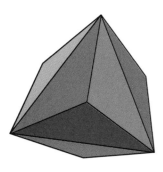

Triakis Tetrahedron

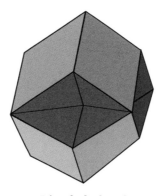

Dimpled Rhombic Dodecahedron

Triakis Cube

Truncated Tetrahedron

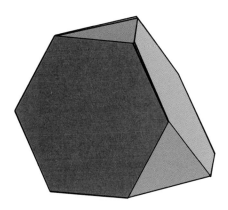

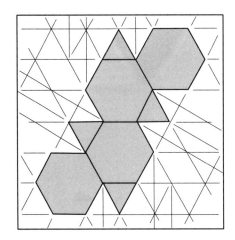

The truncated tetrahedron is an Archimedean solid composed of four triangles and four hexagons. The layout shows odd symmetry.

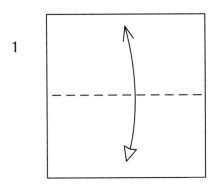

1

Fold and unfold.

2

Fold on the left.

3

Unfold.

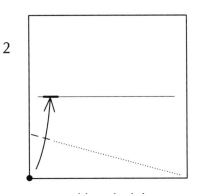

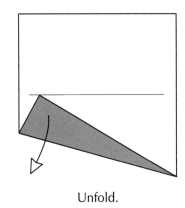

4

1. Fold and unfold on the left.
2. Fold to the dot.
Rotate 180°.

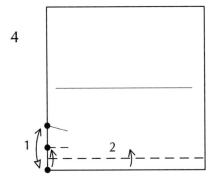

5

Repeat steps 2–5.

6

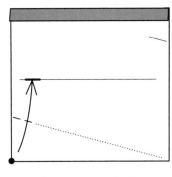

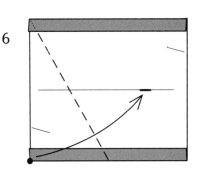

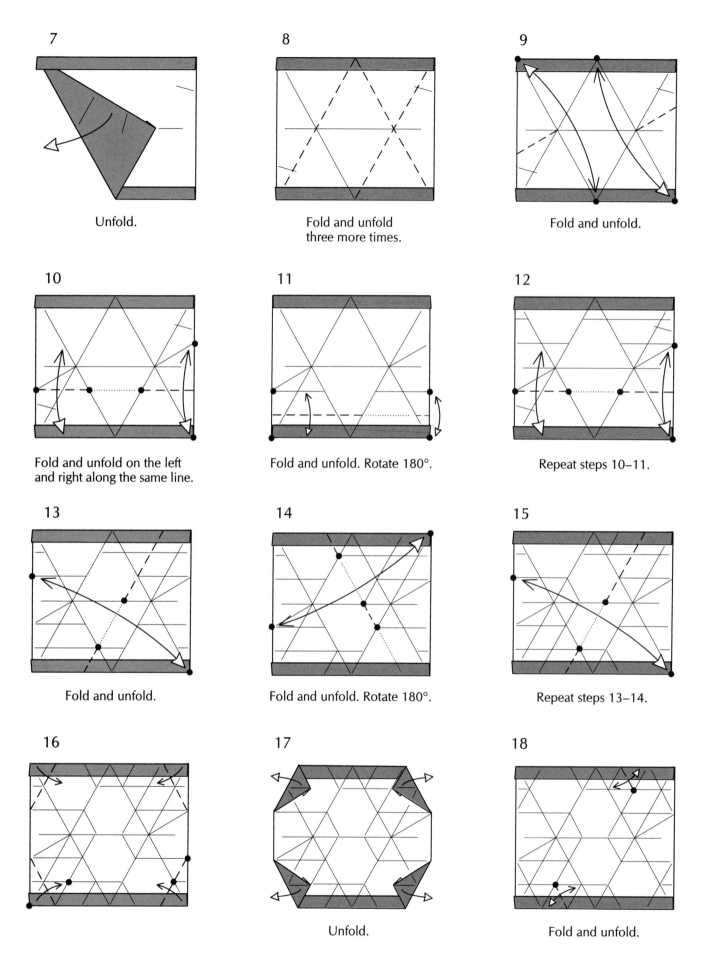

7

Unfold.

8

Fold and unfold
three more times.

9

Fold and unfold.

10

Fold and unfold on the left
and right along the same line.

11

Fold and unfold. Rotate 180°.

12

Repeat steps 10–11.

13

Fold and unfold.

14

Fold and unfold. Rotate 180°.

15

Repeat steps 13–14.

16

17

Unfold.

18

Fold and unfold.

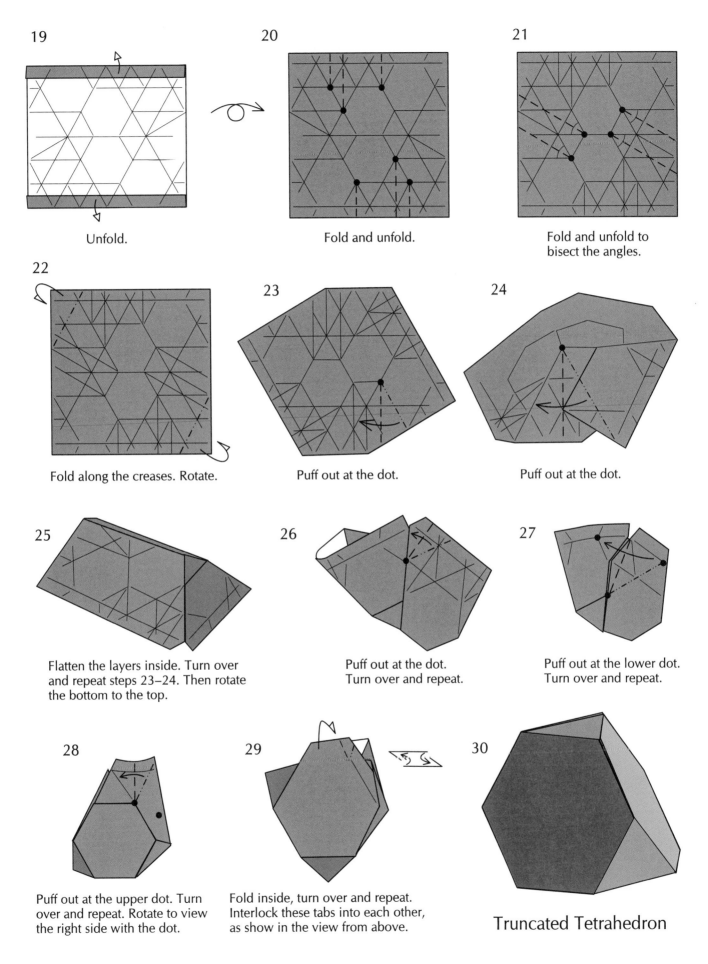

19

Unfold.

20

Fold and unfold.

21

Fold and unfold to bisect the angles.

22

Fold along the creases. Rotate.

23

Puff out at the dot.

24

Puff out at the dot.

25

Flatten the layers inside. Turn over and repeat steps 23–24. Then rotate the bottom to the top.

26

Puff out at the dot. Turn over and repeat.

27

Puff out at the lower dot. Turn over and repeat.

28

Puff out at the upper dot. Turn over and repeat. Rotate to view the right side with the dot.

29

Fold inside, turn over and repeat. Interlock these tabs into each other, as show in the view from above.

30

Truncated Tetrahedron

Triakis Tetrahedron

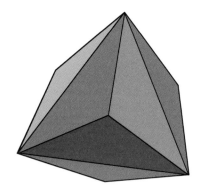

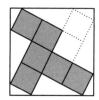

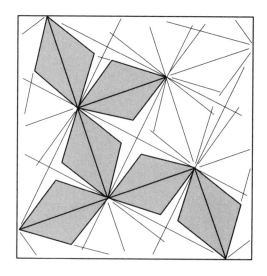

The triakis tetrahedron is a Catalan solid whose dual is the truncated tetrahedron, an Archimedean solid. It resembles a puffed-out tetrahedron and is composed of twelve isosceles triangles. The sides of each triangle are proportional to 3, 3, and 5.

This design comes from a cube whose layout is shown with the small drawing. This is an example of how polyhedra are related, which can be used for origami design.

1

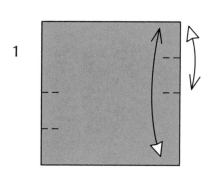

Fold and unfold to divide into fourths.

2

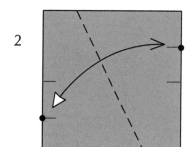

Fold and unfold.

3

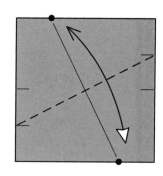

Fold and unfold.

4

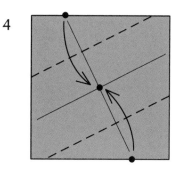

5

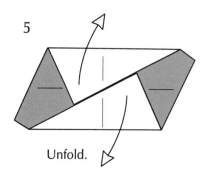

Unfold.

6

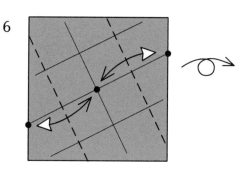

Fold and unfold.

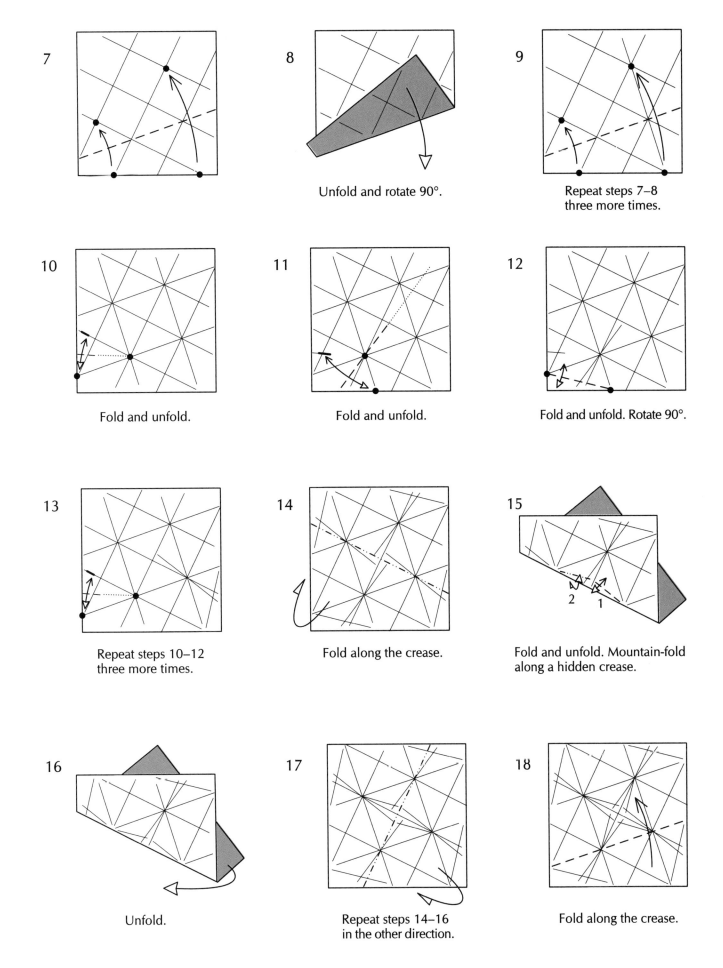

7

8

Unfold and rotate 90°.

9

Repeat steps 7–8
three more times.

10

Fold and unfold.

11

Fold and unfold.

12

Fold and unfold. Rotate 90°.

13

Repeat steps 10–12
three more times.

14

Fold along the crease.

15

2   1

Fold and unfold. Mountain-fold
along a hidden crease.

16

Unfold.

17

Repeat steps 14–16
in the other direction.

18

Fold along the crease.

Triakis Tetrahedron 101

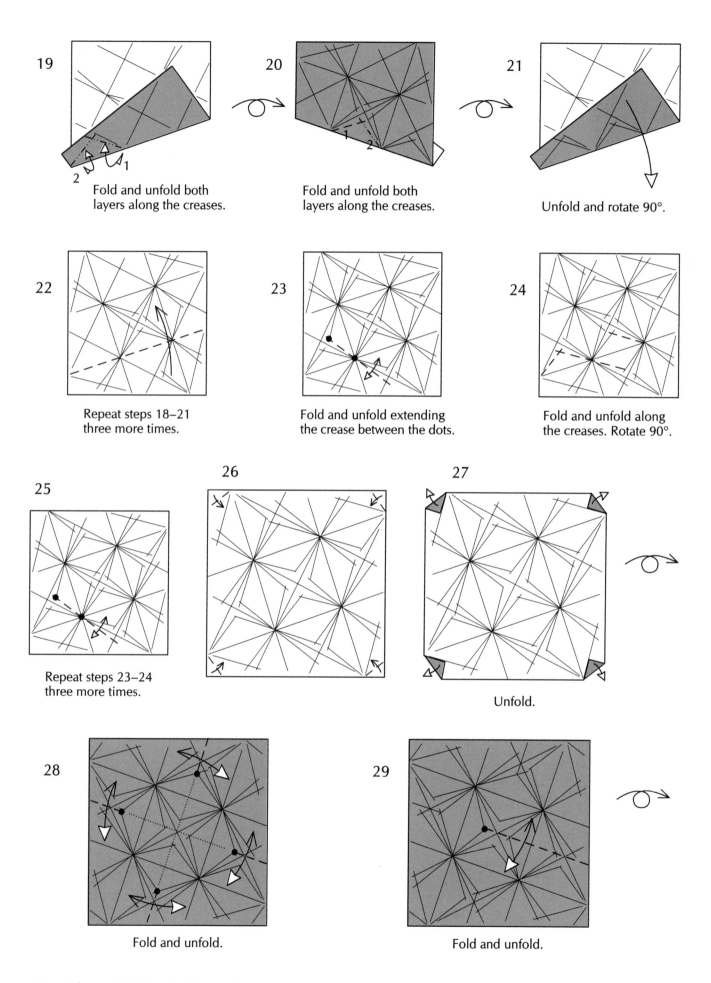

19 Fold and unfold both layers along the creases.

20 Fold and unfold both layers along the creases.

21 Unfold and rotate 90°.

22 Repeat steps 18–21 three more times.

23 Fold and unfold extending the crease between the dots.

24 Fold and unfold along the creases. Rotate 90°.

25 Repeat steps 23–24 three more times.

26

27 Unfold.

28 Fold and unfold.

29 Fold and unfold.

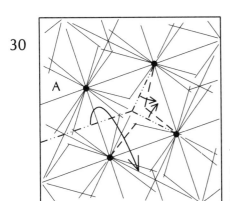

30

The folding will become 3D. Lift up on the long mountain fold line, push in on the two dots on the right and the other two dots will meet.

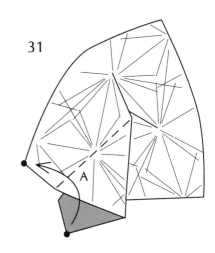

31

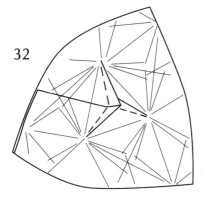

32

Rotate to view the outside.

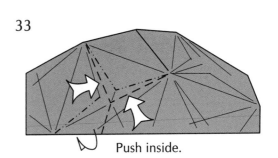

33

Push inside.

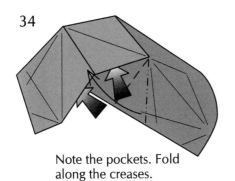

34

Note the pockets. Fold along the creases.

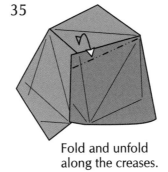

35

Fold and unfold along the creases.

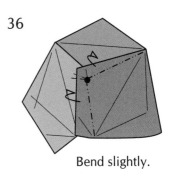

36

Bend slightly.

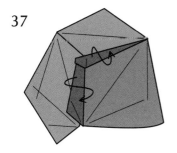

37

Tuck the tabs, shown in a darker shade, into the pockets.

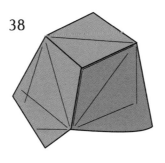

38

Repeat steps 33–37 two more times. One side has more layers. The loose corners meet inside with a twist lock.

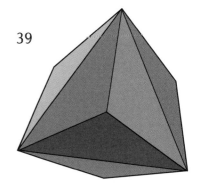

39

Triakis Tetrahedron

Cuboctahedron

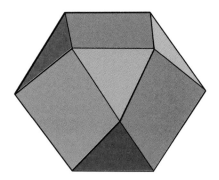

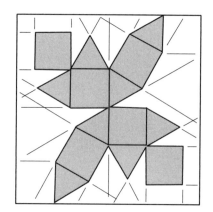

The cuboctahedron, an Archimedean solid, has fourteen sides, six squares and eight equilateral triangles. This design uses odd symmetry.

1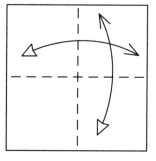

Fold and unfold.

2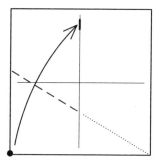

Fold on the left.

3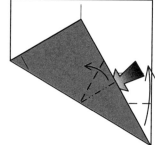

Mountain-fold along the crease for this squash fold.

4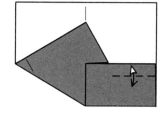

Fold and unfold on the right along a hidden crease.

5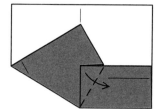

6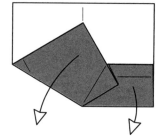

Unfold and rotate 180°.

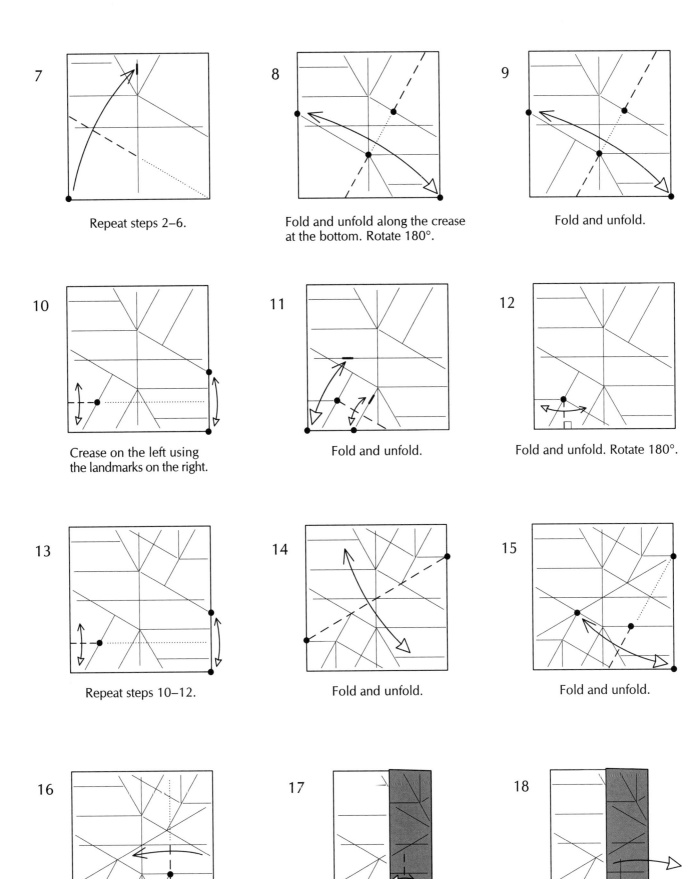

7 Repeat steps 2–6.

8 Fold and unfold along the crease at the bottom. Rotate 180°.

9 Fold and unfold.

10 Crease on the left using the landmarks on the right.

11 Fold and unfold.

12 Fold and unfold. Rotate 180°.

13 Repeat steps 10–12.

14 Fold and unfold.

15 Fold and unfold.

16

17 Fold and unfold along a hidden crease.

18 Unfold.

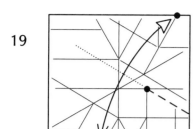

19 Fold and unfold on the right. The upper right corner will meet the bottom edge.

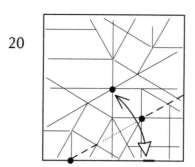

20 Fold and unfold. The bottom edge will meet the center. Rotate 180°.

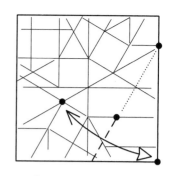

21 Repeat steps 15–20.

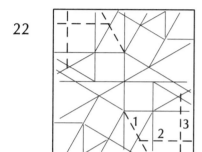

22 Fold and unfold along the creases.

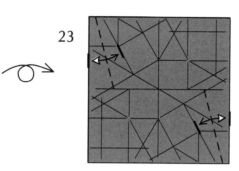

23 Fold and unfold the edges to the creases.

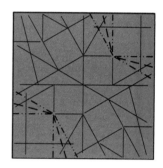

24 Bisect the four angles. Fold and unfold. Mountain-fold along the creases.

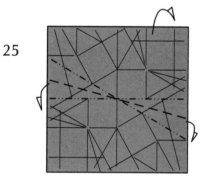

25 Bisect the angles. Mountain-fold along the creases.

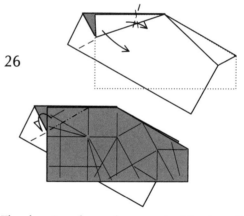

26 The drawing above shows an inside view. This is a spine-lock fold. Turn over and repeat.

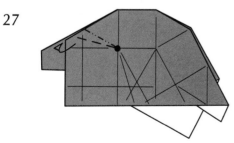

27 Puff out at the dot. To do this fold, the model will become 3D.

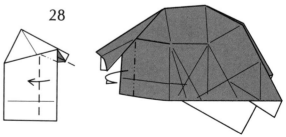

28 The model is 3D. Squash-fold. The small picture shows an inside view if the model is turned around.

29

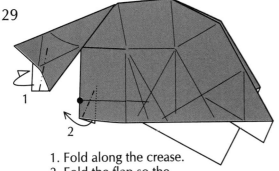

1. Fold along the crease.
2. Fold the flap so the edge meets the dot.

30

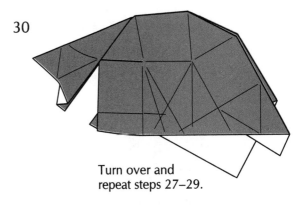

Turn over and repeat steps 27–29.

31

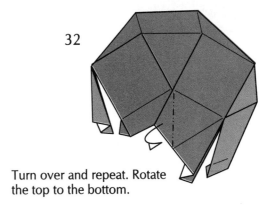

Puff out at the dots. Turn over and repeat.

32

Turn over and repeat. Rotate the top to the bottom.

33

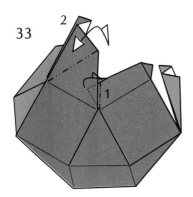

1. Fold behind the flap which is mostly hidden.
2. Fold and unfold.
Turn over and repeat.

34

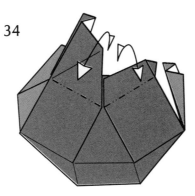

Fold and unfold. Turn over and repeat.

35

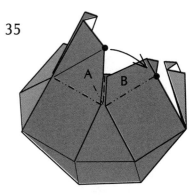

Region A will cover region B. Turn over and repeat.

36

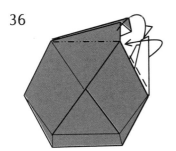

Tuck and interlock the tabs.

37

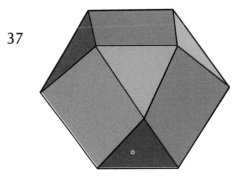

Cuboctahedron

Dimpled Rhombic Dodecahedron

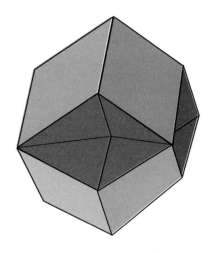

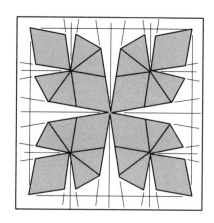

The rhombic dodecahedron is composed of twelve sides, each with diagonals proportional to 1 and √2. For this dimpled form, four sides are sunk. The model uses square symmetry and closes with a twist lock.

The dual of the rhombic dodecahedron is the cuboctahedron.

1

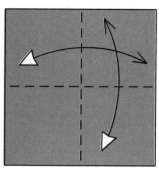

Fold and unfold.

2

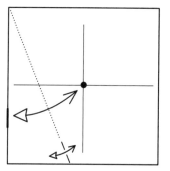

Bring the edge to the center creasing at the bottom. Fold and unfold. Rotate 180°.

3

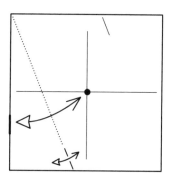

Fold and unfold.

4

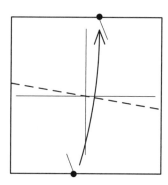

5

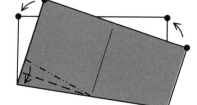

Valley-fold along the crease. Turn over and repeat.

6

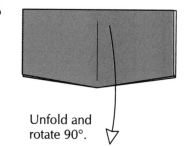

Unfold and rotate 90°.

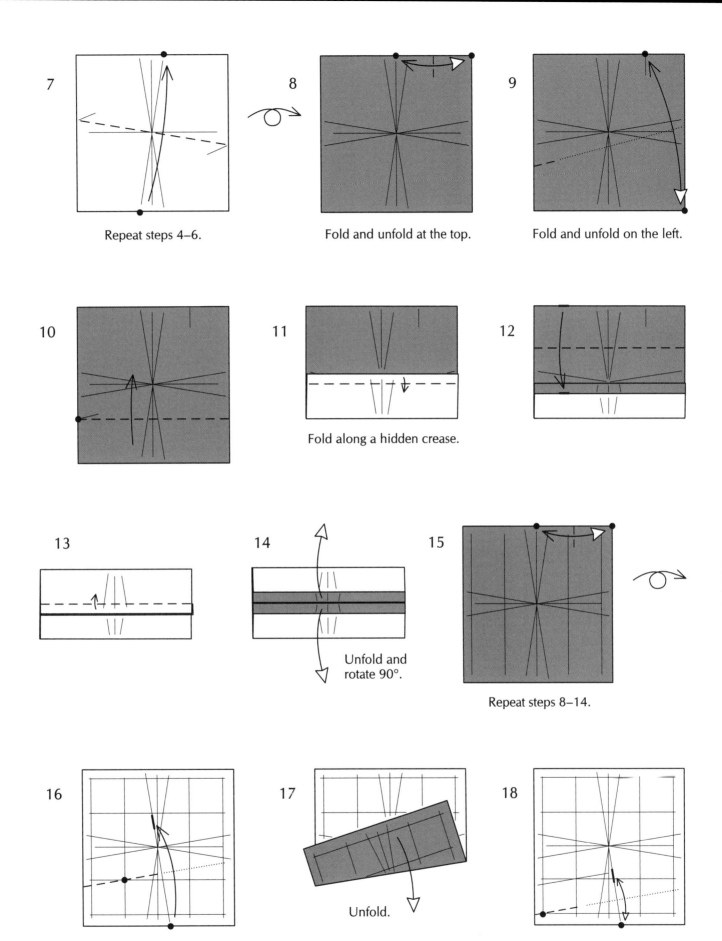

7

Repeat steps 4–6.

8

Fold and unfold at the top.

9

Fold and unfold on the left.

10

11

Fold along a hidden crease.

12

13

14

Unfold and rotate 90°.

15

Repeat steps 8–14.

16

17

Unfold.

18

Fold and unfold on the left.

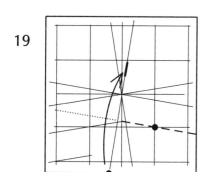

19

Repeat steps 16–18 in the
other direction. Rotate 90°.

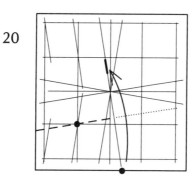

20

Repeat steps 16–19
three more times.

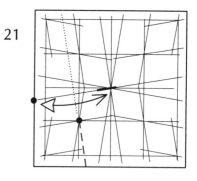

21

Fold and unfold
at the bottom.

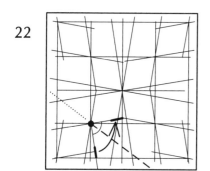

22

Bisect the angle.

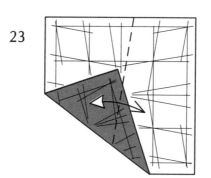

23

Fold and unfold along a
partially hidden crease.

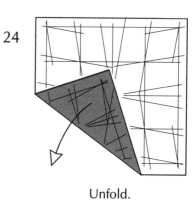

24

Unfold.

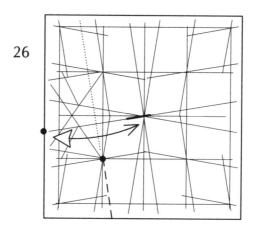

25

Repeat steps 21–24 in the
other direction. Rotate 90°.

26

Repeat steps 21–25
three more times.

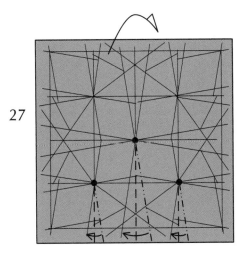

27

Puff out at the dots.

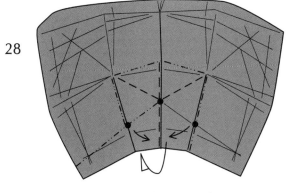

28

Push in at the upper dot.
The other dots will meet.

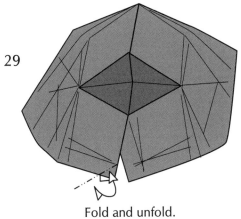

29

Fold and unfold.
Rotate 90°.

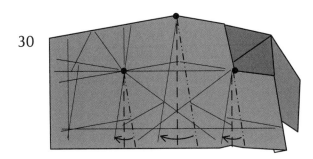

30

Repeat steps 27–29
three more times.

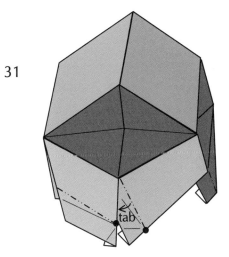

31

tab

Tuck the four tabs
with a twist lock.

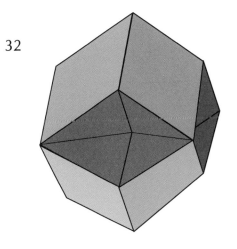

32

Dimpled Rhombic
Dodecahedron

Rhombicuboctahedron

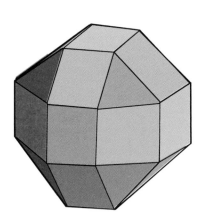

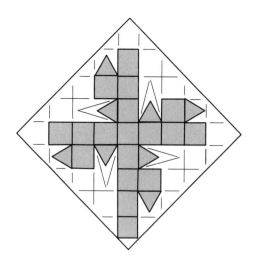

The rhombicuboctahedron has eighteen square faces and eight triangular faces. The paper is divided into tenths. This Archimedean solid makes for a challenging model to fold.

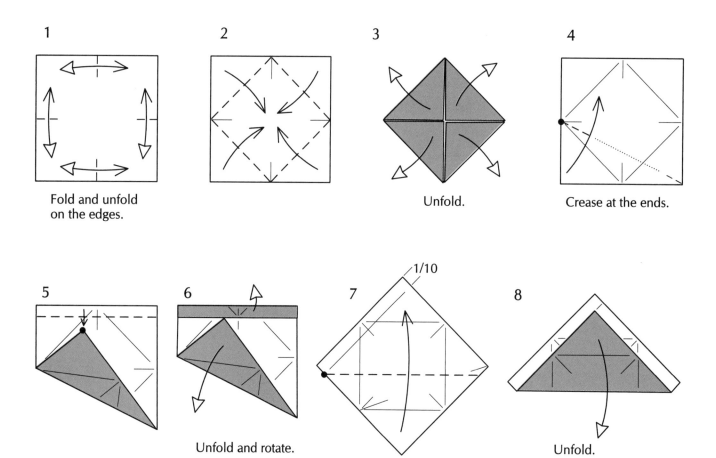

1

Fold and unfold on the edges.

2

3

Unfold.

4

Crease at the ends.

5

6

Unfold and rotate.

7

1/10

The one tenth mark is found.

8

Unfold.

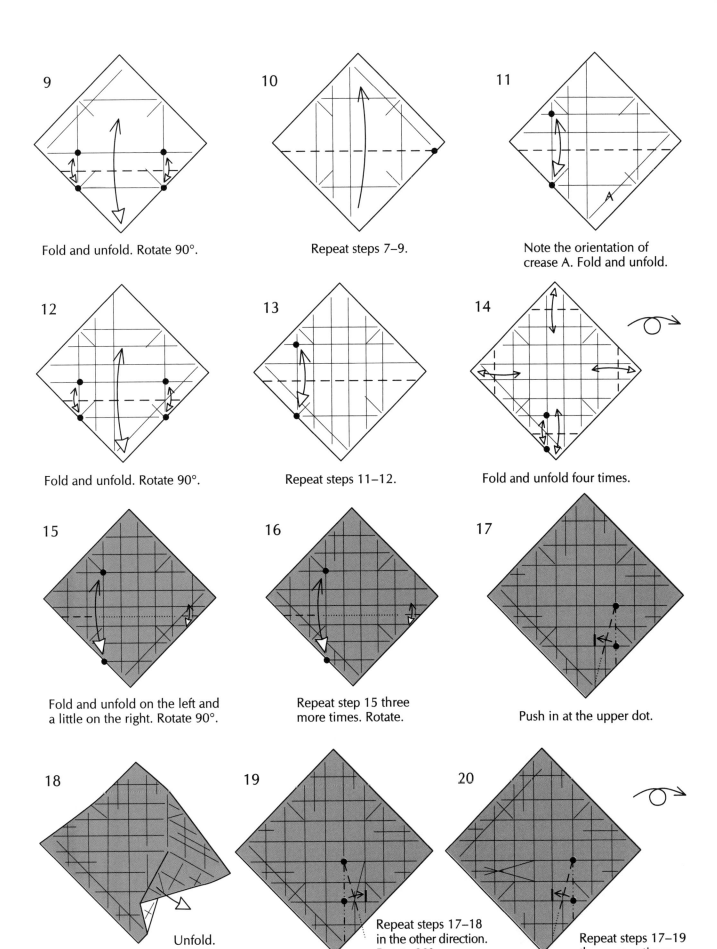

9

Fold and unfold. Rotate 90°.

10

Repeat steps 7–9.

11

Note the orientation of crease A. Fold and unfold.

12

Fold and unfold. Rotate 90°.

13

Repeat steps 11–12.

14

Fold and unfold four times.

15

Fold and unfold on the left and a little on the right. Rotate 90°.

16

Repeat step 15 three more times. Rotate.

17

Push in at the upper dot.

18

Unfold.

19

Repeat steps 17–18 in the other direction. Rotate 90°.

20

Repeat steps 17–19 three more times.

Rhombicuboctahedron 113

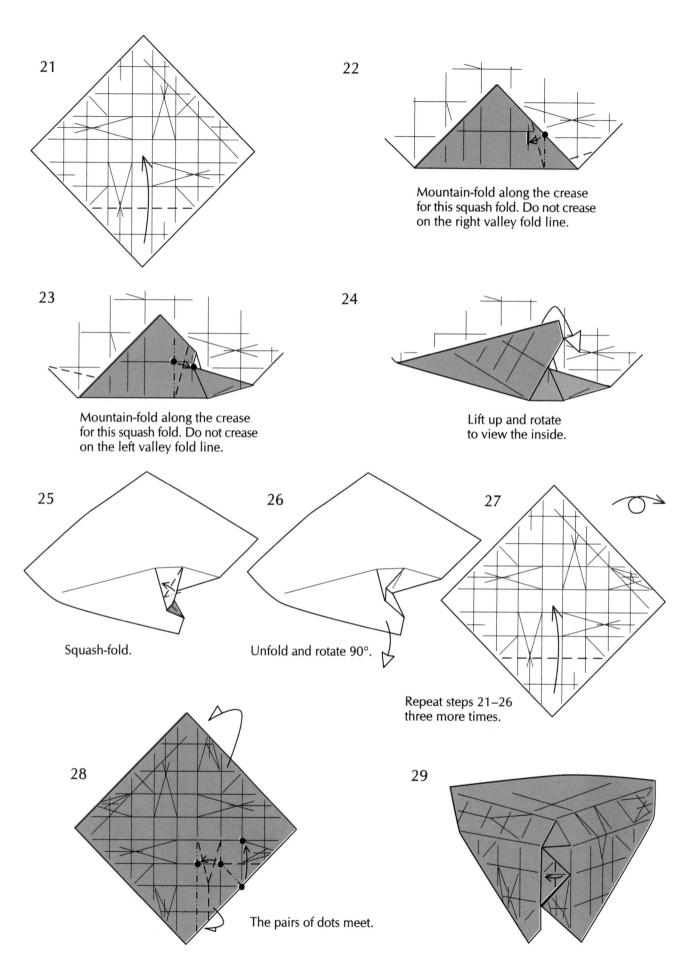

21

22

Mountain-fold along the crease
for this squash fold. Do not crease
on the right valley fold line.

23

Mountain-fold along the crease
for this squash fold. Do not crease
on the left valley fold line.

24

Lift up and rotate
to view the inside.

25

Squash-fold.

26

Unfold and rotate 90°.

27

Repeat steps 21–26
three more times.

28

The pairs of dots meet.

29

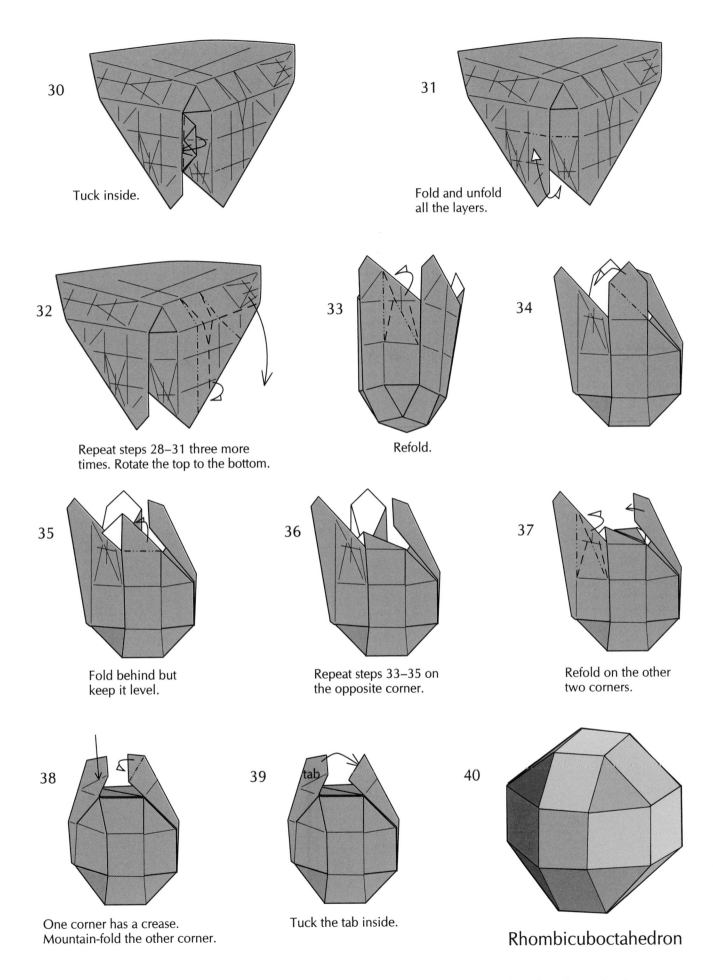

30

Tuck inside.

31

Fold and unfold
all the layers.

32

Repeat steps 28–31 three more
times. Rotate the top to the bottom.

33

Refold.

34

35

Fold behind but
keep it level.

36

Repeat steps 33–35 on
the opposite corner.

37

Refold on the other
two corners.

38

One corner has a crease.
Mountain-fold the other corner.

39

tab

Tuck the tab inside.

40

Rhombicuboctahedron

Triakis Cube

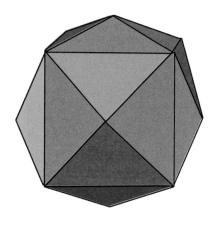

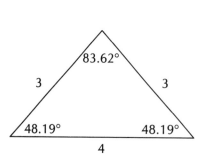

83.62°

3   3

48.19°   48.19°

4

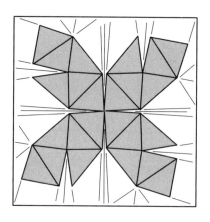

This 24-sided polyhedron is the dual to the truncated octahedron. It resembles a cube where each side extends outward. The sides of each triangle are proportional to 3, 3, and 4. The layout shows square symmetry. Folding unusually thin angles are required for this design.

1
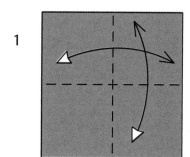

Fold and unfold.

2

Fold and unfold
along the center.

3
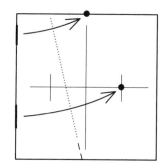

Bring the left edge to the
dots. Crease at the bottom.

4
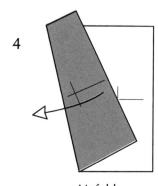

Unfold.

5
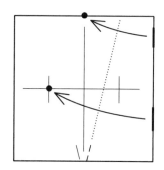

Repeat steps 3–4 in the other
direction. Rotate 180°.

6
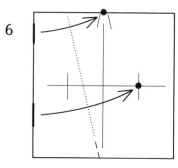

Repeat steps 3–5.

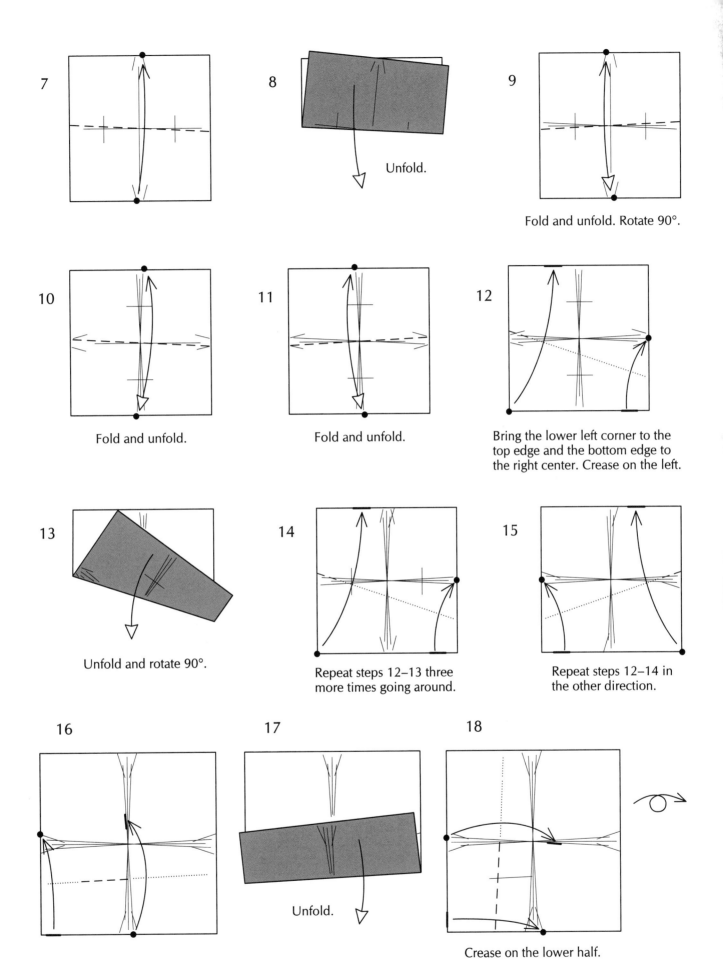

7

8

Unfold.

9

Fold and unfold. Rotate 90°.

10

Fold and unfold.

11

Fold and unfold.

12

Bring the lower left corner to the
top edge and the bottom edge to
the right center. Crease on the left.

13

Unfold and rotate 90°.

14

Repeat steps 12–13 three
more times going around.

15

Repeat steps 12–14 in
the other direction.

16

17

Unfold.

18

Crease on the lower half.

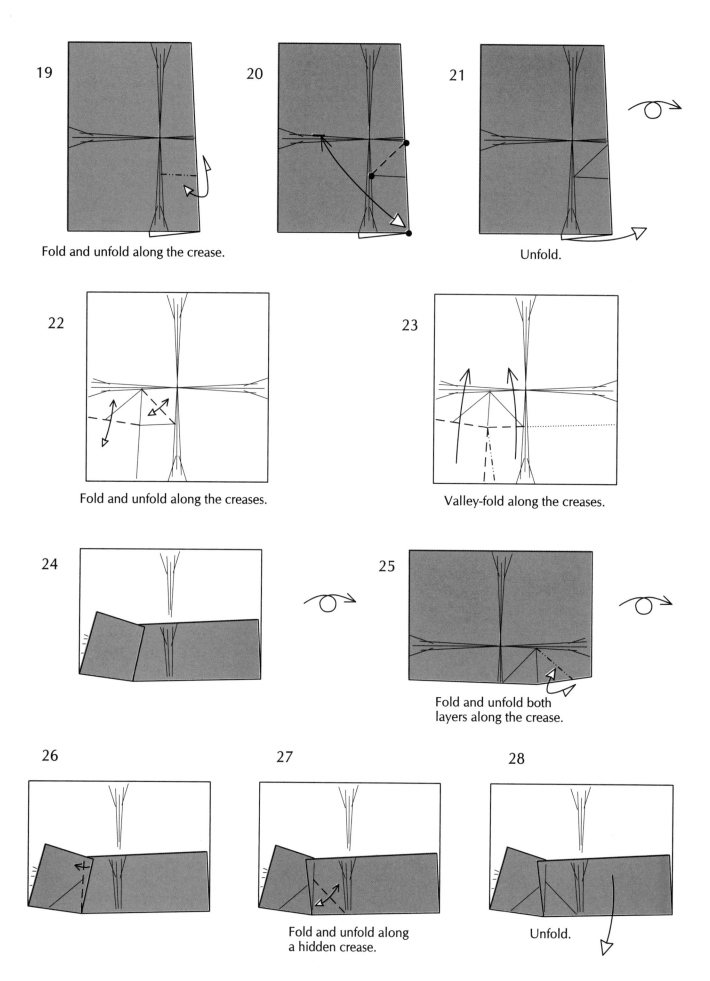

19 Fold and unfold along the crease.

20

21 Unfold.

22 Fold and unfold along the creases.

23 Valley-fold along the creases.

24

25 Fold and unfold both layers along the crease.

26

27 Fold and unfold along a hidden crease.

28 Unfold.

29

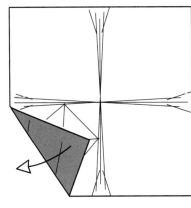

Fold along the crease
between the dots.

30

Fold and unfold along
a hidden crease.

31

Unfold.

32

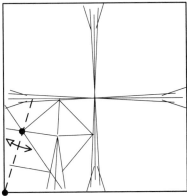

Fold and unfold.

33

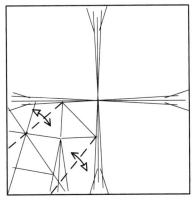

Fold and unfold
extending the creases.

34

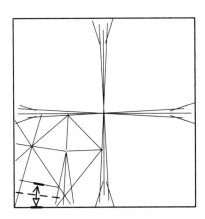

Fold and unfold the bottom
edge to the crease. Rotate 90°.

35

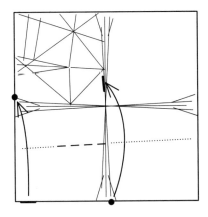

Repeat steps 16–34
three more times.

36

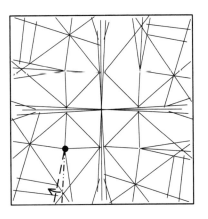

Push in at the dot.

37

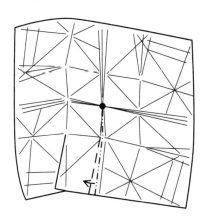

Push in at the dot.

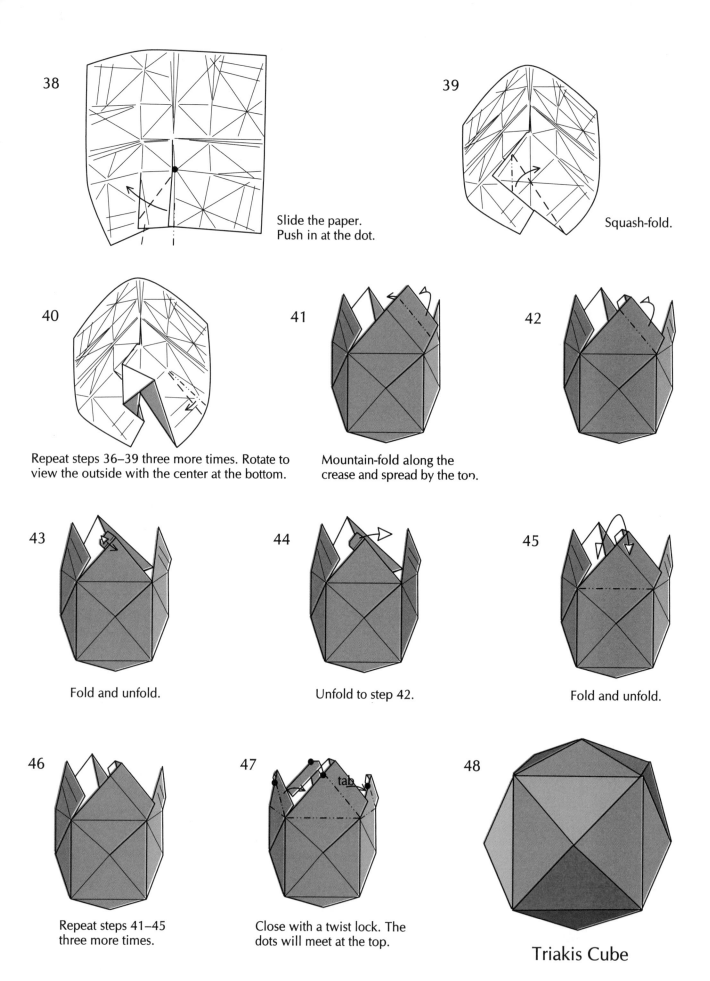

38

Slide the paper.
Push in at the dot.

39

Squash-fold.

40

Repeat steps 36–39 three more times. Rotate to
view the outside with the center at the bottom.

41

Mountain-fold along the
crease and spread by the top.

42

43

Fold and unfold.

44

Unfold to step 42.

45

Fold and unfold.

46

Repeat steps 41–45
three more times.

47

tab

Close with a twist lock. The
dots will meet at the top.

48

Triakis Cube